How to Become an Occupational Psychologist

The business world is increasingly aware of the value of psychology. And as organizations turn to Occupational Psychologists to help build positive, effective and healthy workplaces, so an increasing number of psychologists are choosing this fascinating area of work to make their impact as a practitioner. But how do you qualify, and what is the job really like?

How to Become an Occupational Psychologist is the first book to provide an overview of the educational and professional pathway to becoming an Occupational Psychologist. Providing a summary of what the role entails, and what training is required, it is written by people currently working in the field, sharing not only what helped them in their careers, but also what they learned along the way.

Occupational Psychologists, Professor Stephen A. Woods and Professor Binna Kandola, have a wealth of experience in both education and consultancy, which they have brought to life in this edition, a perfect companion for anyone interested in moving into this exciting profession.

Stephen A. Woods is a Professor of Work and Organisational Psychology at the University of Surrey, UK.

Binna Kandola is MD of Pearn Kandola Ltd and has visiting professorships at Aston Business School and Leeds Business School, UK.

D1447662

How to Become a Practitioner Psychologist

Series Editor: David Murphy, University of Oxford

Psychology remains one of the most popular choices for an under-graduate degree, whilst an increasing number of postgraduate courses are directed either towards further academic study in a sub-discipline, or a career in applied practice. But despite the growing numbers of people interested in a career in psychology, from A-level students to those looking for a career change, the various pathways to entry into the profession are not necessarily obvious.

The *How to Become a Practitioner Psychologist* series of books is aimed at providing a clear, accessible and reader-friendly guide to the routes available to becoming a practitioner psychologist. Providing both information and advice, including testimonials from those recently qualified, the series will include a title for each of the 7 domains of psychology practice as regulated by the Health and Care Professions Council.

Each book in the series will provide an invaluable introduction to anyone considering a career in this fascinating profession.

David Murphy, FBPsS FRSA, is the 2019–20 President of the British Psychological Society (BPS). He is past chair of the BPS Professional Practice Board and former Director of the BPS Division of Clinical Psychology Professional Standards Unit. He has worked in the National Health Service for nearly 30 years, during which time he worked across many different medical specialties, led a clinical health psychology and neuropsychology service in a large acute hospital trust in London and went on to became Director of the Oxford Institute of Clinical Psychology Training.

How to Become an Occupational Psychologist
Stephen A. Woods and Binna Kandola

How to Become an Educational Psychologist
Jeremy Swinson and Phil Stringer

How to Become a Sport and Exercise Psychologist
Martin Eubank and David Tod

How to Become a Counselling Psychologist
Elaine Kasket

www.routledgetextbooks.com/textbooks/howtopsy/default.php

How to Become an Occupational Psychologist

Stephen A. Woods and
Binna Kandola

Routledge
Taylor & Francis Group

LONDON AND NEW YORK

First published 2019
by Routledge
2 Park Square, Milton Park, Abingdon, Oxon OX14 4RN

and by Routledge
52 Vanderbilt Avenue, New York, NY 10017

Routledge is an imprint of the Taylor & Francis Group, an informa business

© 2019 Stephen A. Woods and Binna Kandola

British Library Cataloguing-in-Publication Data
A catalogue record for this book is available from the British Library

Library of Congress Cataloging-in-Publication Data
A catalog record for this book has been requested

ISBN: 978-1-138-67608-4 (hbk)
ISBN: 978-1-138-67609-1 (pbk)
ISBN: 978-1-315-56026-7 (ebk)

Typeset in Galliard
by Apex CoVantage, LLC

Visit the companion website: www.routledgetextbooks.com/textbooks/
howtopsy/

Printed in the United Kingdom
by Henry Ling Limited

Contents

Foreword

A note on the title "Occupational Psychologist" and this book

Occupational Psychologist is a title peculiar to the United Kingdom. It is a protected title, which means that people who call themselves Occupational Psychologists have met a rigorous standard of training requirements and are registered with the Health and Care Professions Council in the UK as *practitioner psychologists* in the area of Occupational practice.

If you are reading this book and are not developing your career as a psychologist in the UK, but are practicing in the areas of work, business, organizations or human resource management, then you will refer to yourself as a "Work and Organizational Psychologist" in Europe, or an "Industrial and Organizational Psychologist" in the US, and either one of these titles if you work elsewhere in the world.

So is this book for all of the above?

Yes.

This book is about how to be an Occupational Psychologist. Because we (the authors) trained, and are based in the UK, and our book is part of a series on psychology in the UK, we will review in depth how to train as an Occupational Psychologist and attain registered status as a practitioner psychologist.

However, we all also work internationally, and have a wide experience of collaborating with psychologists in other countries and cultures. What we write about the skills and competencies of our profession in this book reflects our beliefs about what is needed to be an effective psychologist in the areas of work and organizations.

The guidance included here on *How to be an Occupational Psychologist* also applies to you if you want to be a work and organizational psychologist in Norway, or a personnel psychologist in South Africa or an industrial and organizational psychologist in Singapore. In our book we will use the title "Occupational Psychologist".

It is our wish that this book helps people training in our field globally. It is intended first and foremost as a guide for people training as psychologists – the next generation of practitioners. Yet, there may be valuable insights for people supervising the training of psychologists in countries where the profession is developing. The UK training route for psychologists is well advanced and effectively regulated, and is likely to be of interest to those designing and establishing regulation and training in their own countries.

Why do we wish this? Simply because we believe that effective Occupational Psychologists have the potential to make a huge contribution in the world. They are concerned with the very lifeblood of society – work, and the organization of work. Psychologists can make the difference between productive and unproductive work, between healthy and unhealthy work and between sustainable and unsustainable work. By making work better, more rewarding, fairer and more sustainable, Occupational Psychologists can have a major impact on societies and economies. In our simple thinking, whatever enhances the training of psychologists also increases their likely impact in these respects.

However you use the book, we hope you enjoy reading it, and more importantly, we hope it helps you to be an effective practitioner. Please tell us how you used the book, by contacting us.

Introduction

David Murphy – Series Editor

Welcome!

First, I would like to welcome you to this book, which is one of a series of seven titles each of which focuses on a different type of practitioner psychologist registered as a professional in the UK. One of the things that has always appealed to me about psychology is its incredible diversity; even within my own primary field of clinical psychology there is a huge range of client groups and ways of working. The books in this series are all written by practitioner psychologists who are not only experts in, but also hugely enthusiastic about, each of their areas of practice. This series presents a fascinating insight into the nature of each domain and the range of activities and approaches within it and also the fantastic variety there is across the different areas of practice. However, we have also made sure that we have answered the practical questions you may have such as *"How long does it take to train?"*, *"What do I need to do to get on a training course?"* and *"How secure will my income be at the end of it all?"*. We very much hope that this book will be interesting and answer all your questions (even ones you didn't know you had!) and further information and resources are available on our series website (www.routledgetextbooks.com/textbooks/howtopsy/default.php).

Psychology as a profession

Psychology is still a relatively young profession compared to many long-established professions such as law, medicine, accounting, etc., however it has grown incredibly rapidly over the last few decades. One of the first people to use the title "Psychologist" in a professional context was Lightner Witmer who, only just over a hundred years ago, established what is widely recognized as the world's first psychology clinic in Pennsylvania. Witmer came to study psychology after taking a degree in economics and postgraduate studies in political science and then working for a time as a school teacher. He went on to study experimental psychology at the University of Pennsylvania and then at a famous laboratory in Leipzig in Germany. He subsequently became a pioneer the application of experimental psychology ideas to the treatment of children with specific learning and speech difficulties.

At the beginning of the twentieth century these early psychologists saw great possibilities in applying psychological concepts to help people achieve their potential. However, even they could scarcely imagine the scale and range of applications of psychology that would exist by the beginning of the twenty first century. Psychologists now have well-established roles in schools, mental and physical health services, prisons, police and security services, multi-national companies, sport training centres; essentially almost anywhere where there is a focus on understanding and changing human behaviour, which, of course, is pretty much everywhere!

This book, along with the other six titles in the series, is intended to provide people who are at the beginning of their careers, or those who are thinking about making a change, an insight into the different areas of professional psychology. We hope that you will not only gain an overview of the specific domain of psychology entails, but also a sense of what it is like to work as a practitioner on a day-to-day basis. We also aim to explain how to become qualified to practice in the area of professional psychology, right from school until being fully qualified. Furthermore, we hope to provide an idea of how careers in the different areas of psychology can develop over time and how the profession of psychology might change as it continues to develop in the future.

Studying psychology at school or college

One thing that many people love about psychology is just how broad it is. As an academic discipline it encompasses physiological workings of the brain and the nervous system, how we perceive sounds and language, how we make decisions and the treatment mental health problems, to name just a few areas. In recent years psychology has become the second most popular first degree subject at UK universities, indeed, figures from the Higher Education Statistical Agency (HESA) show that a total of 80,000 students were studying, either full-time or part-time, for a first degree in psychology in the academic year 2016–17.

Psychology has also become not only a popular A-level choice but also increasingly an option at GCSE level. It is therefore now possible to take the first step on a career journey in psychology at an early age, and, if you are considering A-levels or GCSE subjects, we would certainly encourage you to look at psychology options if they are offered at your school. However, it is by no means required to have studied psychology at either GCSE or A-level in order to follow a career in psychology. If psychology isn't offered at your school, or you opt to go for other subjects, this won't stop you going on to become a psychologist, if you decide that this is what you would like to do. On the other hand, contrary to some myths, psychology is considered a valid A-level choice for many other degrees apart from psychology, indeed it is listed as a "preferred subject" by University College London in their general list of A level subject choices www.ucl.ac.uk/prospective-students/undergraduate/application/requirements/preferred-a-level-subjects

The only GCSE subjects that are specifically required by UK Universities to study psychology are maths and English. A-level Psychology is usually listed as a "preferred" subject but is currently not required by any UK university for entry to a psychology degree course and there is no indication that this will change. Therefore, overall, our advice would be that psychology is an interesting subject choice which can provide a good foundation for further study in psychology, or other subjects. However, psychology at A-level is by no means essential for a career as a psychologist, so we recommend basing the decision on what your strengths and interests are and also what subjects are required for any other degree options you want to keep open to you.

Studying psychology at university

The first compulsory step on the road to a psychology career is attaining "*Graduate Basis for Chartered Membership*" of the British Psychological

Society commonly known as "GBC" (in the past this was called "Graduate Basis for Registration" or "GBR" for short). You will see this referred to a number of times in this book and the other titles in the series. The British Psychological Society (BPS) is the professional body and learned society for psychology in the United Kingdom. It was established in 1901 to promote both academic and applied psychology and currently has over 60,000 members, making it one of the largest Psychological Societies in the world. There are two possible routes to attaining Graduate Basis for Chartered Membership of the British Psychological Society on the basis of UK qualifications.

The most common route is to complete an undergraduate degree in psychology that is accredited by the BPS; a lower 2nd class degree classification or above is required for GBC. This doesn't need to be a single honours degree in psychology; it can be a joint degree with another subject. However, in order to be accredited it has to cover a core curriculum that is specified by the BPS and the provision must meet certain other standards. At the time of writing there are 578 BPS-accredited undergraduate courses offered at 126 different higher education Institutions within the UK. Many are of these courses are general psychology degrees however some focus more on specific domains such as forensic psychology, health psychology, abnormal psychology, sport psychology, business psychology and so forth. About a third of all accredited undergraduate programmes are offered as a psychology combined with another subject, and the array of possible options is extensive including; business, English literature, education, maths, history, philosophy, physics, zoology and criminology, to name but a few. This range of choice could be a bit overwhelming, but, it is important to bear in mind that virtually all psychology degrees do offer a significant choice of options within them, so two students doing the same generic psychology degree at the same institution may actually take quite a different mix of courses, albeit still with the same core psychology components. Moreover, it is also important to remember that even if the title of a degree appears very specific, the course will still cover the same core psychology content, if it is BPS-accredited.

For a career in professional psychology, the most important issue is attaining GBC, the subtle differences in the individual course content are far less important. Our advice would be to consider all the factors that are important to you about the choice of university and the psychology course rather than getting too focused on the specific content of a course. You may wish to do a degree that allows you to specialize in the area of psychology that you are particularly interested in, and of course that's fine. However, in reality, all postgraduate professional training courses need to cater for people with a range of different psychology backgrounds, so whilst having done specialized options at undergraduate level might provide a good foundation to build on, it's very unlikely to mean you can jump ahead of those who didn't do those options at undergraduate level.

My own experience was that I did a joint degree with psychology & zoology (I have to confess that I wasn't really sure what psychology was when I was choosing so I hedged my bets!). Fairly early on I became interested in clinical psychology, but I still got a great deal out of studying other subjects that weren't anything to do with clinical psychology, including many of the zoology subjects. In my final year, I did an option in vertebrate paleontology (better known as the study of dinosaurs!) mainly because it sounded interesting. In fact, it turned out to be one of the most stimulating and useful courses I have ever studied, and the lecturer was one of the best teachers I ever had. I learned how to interpret inconclusive evidence by using careful observation and deduction, rather than jumping to conclusions, and that generic skill has been very useful throughout my clinical psychology career. So my personal advice would be not too feel under any pressure to specialize in a particular branch of psychology too soon. I suggest you choose degree options because they are stimulating and well taught, *not* because you think they will look good on your CV. In reality, if you are applying for professional psychology training courses, what will stand out more on your CV will be really good grades which come from being highly engaged and developing a thorough understanding of the areas you are studying.

Some psychology programmes offer a "professional placement year" within the degree. Such courses are often marketed on the basis that graduates have a higher employment rate on graduation, however it is important to bear in mind that you will also be graduating a year later than people on a three-year course, and during the placement year most people will be receiving little or no pay and still paying fees (albeit at a reduced rate) to the university. My own personal opinion is that degrees with professional placements don't necessarily offer a significant advantage overall. On the one hand, if the course does have well-established placement opportunities, this can make it easier to get that first step on the ladder; however, there are many opportunities for getting postgraduate experience relevant to professional psychology some of which are voluntary but many of which are paid.

As well as choosing a specific course, you will also need to choose individual universities to apply to. A detailed consideration of the different universities offering undergraduate psychology programmes is beyond the scope of this series but there is a great deal of information freely available on the web (starting with the UCAS website) and from schools and colleges. It is true to say, however, that universities do vary somewhat and, of course, the area in which they are located is also a factor to consider. The Unistats website (www.unistats.com) is the official website providing data gathered from the National Student Survey and other independent sources which can be used for comparing universities and individual courses. One particular issue that prospective applicants can be confused about is what is meant by a university being in the "Russell Group" and what the significance of this is. The Russell Group is a self-selected association of 24 research-intensive universities across the United Kingdom that was formed in 1994. Although they only account for 15% of all UK Higher Education Institutions, Russell Group universities receive nearly 80% of all UK research funding. However, it does not follow that it is always better to do your psychology degree at a Russell Group university; indeed some of the most highly rated universities for psychology, such as The University of Bath and The University of St Andrews, were not members of the Russell Group at the time of writing. Whilst it is understandable to think that going for a well-known name or the Russell Group "brand-name" must be a safe bet, in order to find the best fit for YOU, there really is no alternative to doing bit of research into individual universities, and the specific course options they offer, and then going to visit to get the feel of the institution and the local area. After all, you will be investing three (or in some cases four) years in your life in this decision, so although it's certainly not something to stress out excessively about, it is worth putting a bit of time into.

Once you have chosen universities and specific courses you wish to apply for, you will need to apply via the University College Admissions Service (UCAS) website (www.ucas.com). This site contains a great deal of advice and you should also access advice about applying from your school or college. One of the things you will be required to do is to submit a personal statement (PS). The UCAS website has comprehensive general information about writing a personal statement including a mind map and worksheet. The key principles of writing a PS are the same regardless of what course you are applying for, i.e. demonstrating you understand what the subject is about, conveying why you are interested in it and demonstrating that you have the skills required to successfully complete the course and make a positive contribution to the learning process. Providing evidence of things you have done which demonstrate your interest, enthusiasm and your abilities will inevitably carry more weight than simply saying "I am passionate about psychology". Furthermore, admissions tutors will also pay attention to how well-structured and well-written your personal statement itself is, since academic writing ability is important to success as a psychology undergraduate. If at this stage you are particularly interested in one career path within professional psychology then you will certainly want to mention this, although it would also be helpful to demonstrate that you understand what the career path involves and that an undergraduate degree is one step towards this. Sometimes people's own experience of mental health or emotional difficulties or that of a close friend or family member has influenced their interest in psychology and/or pursuing a career in psychology. Again, don't feel shy about mentioning this, although only if you feel comfortable doing so. However, don't lose sight of the purpose of the PS and what an admissions tutor will be looking for; lived experience can really help to understand the perspective of people with psychological difficulties but you will also need to cover the other skills required. Furthermore, since psychology is such a broad subject, it's important to bear in mind that you will need to study a whole range of topics most of which will be unrelated to any one specific psychological problem. The Which? University website has a useful article about writing a PS for a psychology degree application (https://university.which.co.uk/advice/personal-statements/personal-statement-advice-psychology-students)

If you are studying for, or have completed, a psychology degree at a University outside of the UK, then your course will not have been accredited by the BPS (at the time of writing the BPS does accredit a small number of undergraduate programmes delivered outside the UK but these have to be awarded by a UK university). However, it is possible to apply for GBC on the basis of a psychology degree undertaken anywhere in the world and the applications are assessed on an individual basis to establish whether the criteria are met (for further information see the www.bps.org.uk/membership/graduate-membership).

People who have done a first degree other than psychology (or those whose psychology degree did not meet the criteria for GBC) can still pursue a career in professional psychology, this route involves attaining GBC by doing a conversion course. At the time of writing there were 78 BPS-accredited conversion courses in the UK. Most of these lead to an MSc, although some lead to a graduate diploma; most are quite general in their content and are titled simply "Psychology" or "Applied psychology", whereas others are more focused in specific areas like child development, mental health or even fashion. However, if they are BPS-accredited, all of these conversion courses will still cover the core psychology curriculum regardless of their title.

Since the core components are common between all BPS-accredited degree programmes, you certainly will not be committing yourself irrevocably to any one area of professional psychology through your choice of psychology undergraduate or postgraduate conversion course. In the clinical psychology programme that I run, we take people who have a range of different experiences at undergraduate level, and some who did different first degrees altogether. Of course, when you come to postgraduate qualifications you do have to make more fundamental choices about the area of psychology you wish to focus on.

The different areas of psychology practice

The authors of each of the seven books in the series are, as you would expect, experts in, and very enthusiastic about, their own area of psychology practice, and the rest of this book will focus pretty much exclusively on this specific area. Our aim across the series is to provide information about what is each domain is about, what it is like to work in this area on a day-to-day basis and what the route to become qualified is like. What we have not done, and indeed could not do, is say which one of the domains is "best". The answer is that there is no one "best" type of psychologist, instead we hope you will be able to find which area of practice seems to fit your own interests and strengths best. This can be difficult and we would encourage you to keep an open mind for as long as you can; you might be surprised to find that an area you hadn't really thought much about seems to be a good fit.

Once you have identified an area of practice that seems to fit you best, we would certainly recommend that you try and meet people who work in that area and talk to them personally. Even after you have embarked on postgraduate training in a particular field, don't feel it's too late to explore other areas. Indeed, there are areas of overlap between the different domains so that psychologists with different training backgrounds might well end up working in a similar area. For instance, clinical and counselling psychologists often work together in psychological therapy services in the NHS, whereas health psychologists and occupational psychologists might work alongside each other in implementing employee health programmes.

My own journey in professional psychology started with my degree in psychology & zoology and led onto postgraduate training in clinical psychology and then working in the National Health Service. However, my journey also included going on to become registered as a health psychologist and a clinical neuropsychologist, and I went on to do management training and becoming a senior manager in the NHS before moving into clinical psychology training and then research in leadership development. Over the years, I have worked alongside colleagues from all of the domains at various times, particularly through roles with the British Psychological Society. I have been fascinated to learn even more about other domains through editing this series and, of course, as psychology is still such a young and dynamic field new developments continue to emerge – you may become a Lightmer Witmer for the twenty first Century – pioneering a new application of psychology that no-one has even thought of yet! I would therefore encourage you to think carefully about your career direction. However, whether your psychology "career" lasts just for the duration of this book, or for the rest of your working life, I would encourage you to maintain an open curious mind, in the words of one of my favourite sayings, "*It is better to travel well than to arrive*". We hope this book, and others in the series, will be of help to you wherever your own unique career journey takes you!

2 | Is Occupational Psychology the right career for you?

What is an Occupational Psychologist?

It is helpful to begin with a definition of what is Occupational Psychology or Work and Organizational Psychology. Woods and West (2014) have defined it as follows:

Work and Organizational Psychology is the study of people and their behaviour at work, and of the organizations in which people work; Work Psychologists develop psychological theory and apply the rigour and methods of psychology to issues that are important to businesses and organizations, in order to promote and advance understanding of individual, group and organizational effectiveness at work, and the well-being and satisfaction of people working in or served by organizations.

An Occupational Psychologist is therefore a practitioner psychologist who works with businesses and organizations to address issues and solve problems that are relevant to them. Key features of the role of Occupational Psychologist are:

1   Application of psychological theory, rigour and methods as an approach to working with businesses and organizations.
2   Working across levels of analysis in an organizations, considering individual, groups and teams, and whole organizations.
3   A focus on dual outcomes of their work: individual, group and organizational effectiveness on the one hand, and the well-being and satisfaction of people working in or affected by organizations on the other (with neither being compromised by the other).

As we have noted earlier, the title "Occupational Psychologist" indicates that a person is registered with the Health and Care Professions Council in the UK. Occupational Psychologists have usually trained in the UK and are regulated in the UK. That means that they have followed a specific pathway of training and preparation. This comprises a) University study and b) a period of practice supervised by a qualified psychologist (referred to as *supervised practice*). Later in this book, we review this training route in depth, and explain the various stages.

In other countries, different titles may be used. Work and organizational psychology is a global profession and the existence of multiple titles simply reflects that practice is set up differently in different countries. For example, in Norway, registration as a work and organizational psychologist requires more extensive training than in the UK. Whereas, in Malaysia, there is no official regulation of titles relating to work and organizational psychology, and so correspondingly, no fixed training route. The situation varies based on national legislative context from country to country.

Coming back to the UK, the Health and Care Professions Council protects the title Occupational Psychologist, but none of the other alternatives. So for example, a Business Psychologist is likely to have studied psychology and work and organizational psychology at University, but may not have trained further through supervised practice after completing their studies.

So how to make sense of this? Our review of the most advanced professional regulatory frameworks would lead us to conclude the following:

1   That the domain of study of all of the titles relating to work and organizational psychology is very consistent; Occupational Psychology programmes in the UK cover very similar foundation knowledge and content to for example, I/O psychology or work and organizational psychology internationally. It would be expected that a University-based programme in management psychology might lean more heavily towards management applications and Human Resource Management (HRM), or that personnel psychology leans more heavily towards assessment of performance or recruitment, but this is against a context of broad similarity.

2   Use of the title "psychologist", to be considered appropriate, should be based on a Doctoral-level qualification (for example, PhD, Practitioner Doctorate, DPhil). Such a qualification could be a research doctorate in the field of work and organizational psychology, or through completion of supervised practice as in the case of the Qualification in Occupational Psychology in the UK, which leads to eligibility to register as an Occupational Psychologist (and is recognized as a doctoral-level qualification). Practitioner doctorates in Occupational Psychology are a means by which people can attain the title of doctor, and register as an Occupational Psychologist.

The versatility of psychology to contribute to work and organizational life provides opportunity for rich and varied professional experiences as an OP. Working with external clients for example, means that it is unlikely that OPs work is ever repetitive. Some examples of typical working days serve to illustrate.

In the first, a client engaged me to develop new assessments of leadership behaviour their organization. It was a technical project in which the key objective was to ensure that the assessments were scientifically robust and that they effectively measured characteristics needed for job performance. Work on a project like this involves very different kinds of working day. On one hand, workshops and focus groups with non-specialists are important to understand the client need and build relationships. An early start in the morning to travel on the train to the client's site in another part of the country provides time for a final recap and review of preparation, project reports, and the materials for the day. After arriving at the client's office, such meetings often start with a short presentation by the psychologist to introduce the objectives of the day. The role then changes to workshop facilitator. Encouraging discussion, moderating the contributions and capturing what people say enables a picture to be built about the issues the client is experiencing and how the assessments will be used as part of the solutions. There is also a social informal aspect to client days like this example. Lunch, or coffee and refreshments are a forum for friendly chatting, all helping to build the mutual trust of the client and consultant psychologist. Social skills are critical.

Away from the workshop, other project days are quite solitary. Working to make sense of information, translate it into something usable, and pore over the quality of the assessment tools – definitions, questionnaire items, rating scales and standard instructions. In this project, three other psychologists participated in a technical workshop to provide critical feedback and comments. Careful review and feedback of solutions amongst professional psychologists retains the science in the work that we do.

A second example illustrates the delivery part of work as an OP. Our field has been effective at sharing the knowledge and tools we have developed in order to make a difference in practice. I often work with practitioners, some of whom are not psychologists, to train them to use psychometric testing in their businesses. The work is that of a *trainer*, designing and delivering learning in a classroom environment, and evaluating whether the group have developed required skills from the sessions. Within a period of 2 months, I have delivered such training in a local medium sized company, within walking distance of my home, in Delhi, to a group comprising participants from India, Democratic Republic of Congo and Oman, and to a group of OP students.

A third example draws on research and written communication skills. A client contacted me about their work in the leadership field. Their speciality was finding temporary leaders to take over responsible roles in organizations, for example to step-in if a company leader or manager left the organization suddenly. They were unable to find good quality evidence on which to base their practices, and although they were successful, they wanted to improve still further. Psychologists are highly effective consumers of research generally, because of our training. We are able to understand the research literature and differentiate good from weak science. Leading a team comprised of another experienced work psychologist, and a recent OP graduate, we undertook research to search the literature for relevant scientific studies, review their findings and make proposals for developing their approach to selection of interim leaders. We also had chance to speak to interim leaders and used psychological interviewing techniques to understand better what made them successful. Our main advantage as psychologists was to be able to explore examples of their experience, focusing on their behaviour, and to code and classify what we heard to provide psychological competency profiles needed for effective leadership in those settings.

These examples hopefully show that the title "Occupational Psychologist" subsumes an array of different expertise areas and work activities. Why do people become one?

Why be an Occupational Psychologist?

There are many different routes of specialism of psychology. The practice specialisms are referred to as areas of applied psychology, each of which apply psychology to a different life domain.

All have value to society, but here is why we are convinced that the psychology of work is especially important.

The vast majority of the world's population work. What they collectively do at work affects all of us. We are pretty certain that you will need to work. And, you will work, most likely, for a significant portion of your life, and a substantial number of your daytime hours will be spent at work.

By focusing on work, Occupational Psychology is relevant to most of us, for most of our lives and a lot of our time.

Being an Occupational Psychologist therefore gives you the opportunity to make an extraordinary impact as a psychologist.

It is also immensely interesting work. Occupational Psychologists typically work on a consultative basis and so work with a variety of different clients, organizations and teams, and work in a range of areas on different unique client problems. Many practitioners also work in different parts of the world, applying their expertise in a variety of cultures internationally. Finding out about, people and their work, and experiencing organizations is almost never dull.

Occupational Psychology is also a profession in which creative and analytical problem solving is needed. This means that the role draws on a wide range of skills, provides stimulating and challenging work, and enables you tremendous freedom in how you approach your work.

Finally, when you create value in yourself and for your clients (something we return to later), the extrinsic rewards and benefits of being an Occupational Psychologist are also excellent.

In summary, Occupational Psychology:

- Enables you to make a big impact as a psychologist
- Is almost always fascinating and interesting work
- Provides variety in many respects
- Is challenging, drawing on many different skills
- Provides autonomy and freedom in how to approach work
- Generally pays well – the extrinsic benefits have high potential

Should you be an Occupational Psychologist?

Having explained why you might want to be an Occupational Psychologist, we now tackle an equally pertinent question: *should* you be an Occupational Psychologist? How do you know it is for you?

You should be an Occupational Psychologist if you are a care about, or are interested in work, organizations and business, *and* want to attain professional status as a psychologist.

Anyone can study or read about work and organizational psychology. In fact, in business schools around the world, business graduates learn about the field. This is a very good thing, because the lessons of work and organizational psychology are relevant for managers and leaders in business, who can apply them day-to-day in their decisions and work activity.

This is different from being a psychologist though. To be an Occupational Psychologist, you first need to have studied psychology to an advanced level at a University, covering the foundations of pure psychology. You next have to specialize as an Occupational Psychologist, which generally means further study, and a period of practice in the field supervised by a qualified psychologist.

You should choose to specialize in Occupational Psychology if you have an interest in working in organizations and businesses to apply psychology to solve problems people face at work.

To be an Occupational Psychologist, you must also want to *master* the profession.

Theories about the way people approach learning tell us about two possible ways of developing skills and knowledge:

- Performance approach, in which people learn in order to perform a certain standard or task.
- Learning approach, in which people are motivated to learn about something as comprehensively as possible for its own sake; that is to master the subject.

Completing the training to be an Occupational Psychologist requires dedication, and a commitment to learning. The practice experience you complete is wide-ranging and extensive, so you really are mastering the profession. Practitioner psychologists also continue to learn through their working lives (it is a professional requirement).

Being an Occupational Psychologist is for you if you want to learn not just to *do* something, but also to *be* something, and to *master* something.

Alongside this general approach to your learning, it is also an advantage to have the following kinds of work interests:

- Investigative and creative problem solving: analysing information, researching and testing assumptions, developing a range of solutions and selecting the most appropriate.
- Enterprise and business: working with organizations and businesses, selling the benefits of the work you do to people who are not psychologists, managing businesses and projects and creating value for clients and for yourself.
- Working with, and for people: working with others at various levels of seniority in organizations to help them address problems they face at work, and caring for the welfare of people at work.

Should you be an Occupational Psychologist? Tick off the following to decide:

- ☐ You want to make an impact in the worlds by applying psychology.
- ☐ You care about, and are interested in work, business and organizations.
- ☐ You prefer to master things you learn about, rather than learn to meet a performance requirement.
- ☐ You value and prefer autonomy and variety in your work.
- ☐ You enjoy investigative, analytical and creative problem solving.
- ☐ You enjoy selling and communicating the value of your expertise to non-psychologists.
- ☐ You enjoy work that has benefit for people socially (i.e. enhancing their welfare or well-being)

If you agreed with the majority of the statements above, then Occupational Psychology could be for you.

3 What do you learn about to be an Occupational Psychologist?

The knowledge domain of Occupational Psychology

What do you need to know about if you want to be an Occupational Psychologist? The knowledge domain of the field is fascinating for those interested in people and their behaviour at work. It brings in influences and content from psychology, organizational behaviour, human resource management and even more widely from sociology and economics for example. Knowledge can include different aspects, for example:

- **Conceptual knowledge:** research, theory and the scientific evidence that acts as the basis of what psychologists do
- **Technical skills:** skills for carrying out research and other problem-solving analysis
- **Practice skills:** skills for carrying out applied work (e.g. selection interviewing, training evaluation, performance assessment)

These different aspects of the knowledge domain are represented in seven key content areas for Occupational Psychology. These areas serve as foundations for study of the profession. For people training, they are reflected in British Psychological Society accredited Master's degree programmes. The seven areas are:

- Psychological assessment at work
- Learning, training and development
- Leadership, engagement and motivation
- Well-being and work

- Work design, organizational change and development
- Research design, advanced data-gathering and analytical techniques
- Applying psychology to organizations

In this Chapter, we will explore each of the seven areas in more detail.

Psychological assessment at work

People are assessed at work for many reasons, such as for recruitment and selection, performance review or promotion. In each case, the task is to accurately measure individual psychological characteristics of the person such as their abilities, skills, traits and competencies, so that decisions about the person's employment can be made based on sound information and evidence.

Psychological assessment practice draws on theories of individual differences and their measurement. Individual differences research has tended to focus on two key aspects of people: their personalities and cognitive abilities (i.e. intelligence). Theories of personality and intelligence therefore form a key part of the knowledge domain in this area (see Box 3.1).

Alongside the conceptual theories are a set of technical concepts that determine how assessments should be carried out according to best practice scientifically, legally and ethically. These concepts are grouped under the heading "psychometrics". The study of psychometrics is concerned with the construction and evaluation of methods of measurement. Key concepts are reliability (the accuracy and stability of assessments) and validity (the extent to which assessments can be shown to measure relevant psychological differences, and to predict organizational behaviour or outcomes like performance at work). Psychometric testing of cognitive ability and personality is an area of research in its own right.

These foundations are built upon in learning about the application of psychometric methods to different assessment techniques such as selection interviewing, work-sample testing, assessment centres, and performance appraisal. The organizational and societal context of assessment is also relevant here. For example, how do we ensure that assessments are fair? Does the use of particular assessments promote or inhibit diversity? These practical challenges are explored more later in the section on Practice of Occupational Psychology.

Knowledge Taster Box 3.1 Personality and intelligence at work

What impact do intelligence and personality have on people's behaviour at work? This is a question that psychologists have researched extensively for decades, amassing a significant evidence base about the influence of individual differences in the workplace.

Intelligence is generally defined as:

> A very general mental capability that, among other things, involves the ability to reason, plan, solve problems, think abstractly, comprehend complex ideas, learn quickly and learn from experience. It is not merely book learning, a narrow academic skill, or test-taking smarts. Rather it reflects a broader and deeper capability for comprehending our surroundings – "catching-on", "making sense" of things, or "figuring out" what to do
>
> Gottfredson (1997, p13)

From this definition, it is apparent why intelligence (or cognitive ability, as it is often termed) might provide an advantage for performance at work. The extent to which assessments of cognitive ability predict workplace performance is referred to as criterion validity, and there are hundreds of studies examining the validity of different tests. However, some of the most important studies in this area are published meta-analyses, which integrate the findings of multiple research studies in the literature to arrive at an overall answer about the extent to which cognitive ability predicts performance. These studies indicate that across almost all jobs, higher cognitive ability is associated with higher job performance.

Why is this? Research points to two key factors. The first is job complexity. The more complex the job, the stronger the association of cognitive ability with performance. The second, related factor is job knowledge. High intelligence enables people to acquire job knowledge more quickly and in greater quantity, resulting in higher performance.

With regards to personality, the vast majority of evidence of the impact of personality assessment on performance is based on personality traits of the Big Five model. The Big Five model comprises five broad dimensions that represent the major domains of personality. They are:

- Extraversion: The extent to which a person is outgoing and sociable versus quiet and reserved
- Agreeableness: The extent to which a person is warm and trusting, versus cold and unfriendly
- Conscientiousness: The extent to which a person is organized and dependable, versus impulsive and disorganized
- Emotional Stability: The extent to which a person is calm and stable, versus neurotic and anxious
- Openness/Intellect: The extent to which a person is imaginative and open to new experiences, versus narrow-minded and unimaginative

Again, meta-analyses in the literature have demonstrated the associations of personality with job performance. People who are conscientious and emotionally stable tend to perform better in most jobs. However, the picture is also more complex. This is because specific traits tend to predict performance in specific jobs. So in jobs that require people to be warm and to get along with others (e.g. service roles), higher Agreeableness tends to be an advantage, in research jobs high Openness is an advantage. Research shows that personality traits tend to predict higher performance when they are relevant to the job. There is not "one personality profile" that predicts performance in all jobs.

Recently, research has extended how we understand the relationships of personality and work. One fascinating finding from this research is that work does have an impact on how our personality develops over time (Woods, Lievens, De Fruyt, & Wille, 2013). Our work becomes part of who we are over the course of our lives.

Learning, training and development

Psychologists have an important contribution to make in the design, delivery and evaluation of training and learning at work. The knowledge base in this area encompasses several key areas:

1   Theories of Learning: Understanding how best to ensure that people learn at work should be based on sound learning theory. Theories in this area come from cognitive psychology and social psychology.
2   Design and Delivery of Learning and Development: There are a wide variety of techniques for facilitating learning and development. These include formal training in classroom-type settings, through self-development and e-learning, to one-to-one focused development through coaching. Psychologists are concerned to understand when, why and how these different techniques result in learning that is applied in the workplace, making an impact on what people do at work.
3   Evaluation of Training and Learning: Questions about the impact of training and learning at work may be answered through applying psychological research techniques. Psychologists have been concerned with understanding how to model the outcomes from training and learning (e.g. learning, attitude change, behaviour change, results and performance; Kirkpatrick 1976) and how to test accurately whether there has been any impact on performance (e.g. applying experimental methods).

More widely, development at work may be viewed in the context of people's entire working lives. Research in psychology in this area concerns how people make choices about occupations that they would prefer to work in, and how they develop through their careers in terms of moving between jobs or levels of seniority.

Knowledge Taster Box 3.2   Training transfer

Why does training and develop succeed or fail in terms of making an impact on organizational effectiveness? This is the question that frames work in the area of training transfer. In this case, transfer refers to the transfer of learning from the training or learning setting to the work setting. Transfer is fundamental to ensuring that investment in staff development has some benefit for organizations and businesses.

In work and organizational psychology, studies have examined factors that determine whether training is transferred. Unsurprisingly, it is not safe to assume that learning is automatically transferred to work. Rather a number of factors must be considered and managed to promote transfer:

- Trainee characteristics: individual differences in cognitive ability, personality and motivation have an impact on whether training is applied.
- Training design: for example, the extent to which the training or development is designed in a way that is appropriate for the skills being learned, and the context in which they are applied.
- Work environment: the extent to which staff are given the opportunity to perform new skills, and the climate in the organization for learning and development

Some key research studies have considered the role of the line manager in facilitating transfer. These studies found that support before the training, and afterwards to identify how the training can be applied, and providing direct support to enable staff to apply learning was beneficial (Salas & Canon-Bowers, 2001). This is particularly the case when training is based on careful and systematic development planning.

Well-being and work

Work has the potential to be a very positive influence on well-being and psychological and physical health, but conversely has the potential to be damaging and unhealthy. Knowledge in this area of work and organizational psychology is concerned with understanding what makes the difference.

Positive well-being at work is represented by a number of concepts. On a basic level, well-being means being happy at work, or satisfied with one's job and work conditions. Job satisfaction is included in a wide array of psychological research studies, with the principle questions around the concept being what influences it, and how it related to job performance (Judge, Thoresen, Bono, & Patton, 2001).

However, well-being is not simply about being satisfied. The positive psychology movement has argued that work should not simply be satisfactory, but actually it should be positive and rewarding. For example, when work is designed in the right way, it provides a number of psychological benefits that are not necessarily provided in other domains of life. These include a sense of meaningfulness about what one contributes to the world, the opportunity to interact socially with others, and to utilize a variety of different skill and capabilities.

Work that includes these kinds of features tends to be more engaging (as described earlier). Engagement at work is positive psychological state representing feelings of being energized and absorbed by work, and dedicated to work activity (Schaufeli, Bakker, & Salanova, 2006).

On the other side of the well-being and engagement are stress and burn out. These are major negative psychological consequences of work. Stress at work occurs when people feel unable to cope with the demands of work, are upset or anxious as a consequence. The process of stress can be modelled as a transaction (Cox, 1993) between work demands and resources. Demands include a number of well-evidenced risk factors for stress at work, for example work overload, role conflict or ambiguity, or interpersonal conflict. Resources include personal resources (skills, abilities) and external (supervisory support, helpful colleagues, effective systems, decision-making control etc). When demands outweigh resources, stress results. When stress at work is chronic and long-term, not only is psychological well-being harmed, but also physical health is damaged by physiological processes and changes that result from stress.

Work and organizational psychologists have led the development of understanding about the causes and consequences of stress at work. They have also led the way on the development of ways to measure and manage stress.

Knowledge Taster Box 3.3 Work-family interface

In what ways might work conflict with family life, and how can conflict be prevented? References to work-life balance are somewhat problematic if one adopts the view that work should be part of life, not somehow separate from it. Rather it makes more sense to consider when the interface of work and family life domains are positive versus problematic. Research in work and organizational psychology has considered this issue from a number of angles, seeking to understand the processes and mechanisms that determine how the interface operates. These are some of their findings:

- Work-family conflict is bi-directional. That means that work may conflict with family life, and also that family life may conflict with work. Demands in ether domain may spill-over into the other.
- Work-family conflict can takes different forms. Time-based conflict happens when the time demands of one domain allow insufficient time to meet demands in the other. Strain-based conflict is when stress in one domain spills over and prevents a person coping adequately with demands in the other. Behaviour-based conflict is when behaviour that is required for effective performance in one domain is ineffective in the other.
- The work-family interface may be positive, not just negative. Models of work-family facilitation describe how resources in one domain can help people cope with demands in the other. For example, social support at home can help people cope with work demands.

Leadership, engagement and motivation

This knowledge area encompasses some major domains of work and organizational psychology theory and research. One is motivation and performance.

Motivation theory is arguably of the most well-developed area conceptually in the field. Theories of motivation explore the various ways in which people are motivated at work. Key mechanisms of motivation include:

- Satisfaction of psychological needs: people seek to satisfy needs such as affiliation, esteem and psychological safety.
- Personal traits that promote motivation: for example, personal need for achievement is a trait-like construct that influences people's drive to succeed.
- goal setting: people typically work harder and direct their effort more effectively when they are set objectives at work (see Knowledge Taster Box).
- Fairness and equity: feeling fairly treated at work in terms of the rewards provided, procedures of management, and interpersonal interactions (i.e. being treated respectfully) promotes motivation.
- Design of jobs that are intrinsically motivating: specific kinds of job characteristics and features tend to promote motivation at work, and ensure it is positive and rewarding.

The literature on motivation is interrelated with two other areas in this knowledge domain. One is performance management. Motivation is a key antecedent of performance, but is not a guarantee. Performance management is about understanding how to measure performance at work, to give feedback to staff about performance, and to manage them such that performance in improved.

The second related aspect is engagement. Engagement is the extent to which people feel dedicated, absorbed and energized by work. Research on engagement is strongly aligned to motivation research, especially in respect of the role of job characteristics and design. Engagement at work is associated by three psychological mechanisms:

- A sense of meaningfulness
- Perception of results and outcomes
- Feeling responsible for the outcomes of work

Research in work and organizational psychology has evaluated the features of jobs that promote these positive states (for example, autonomy, opportunity to use a variety of skills, being able to complete tasks in their entirety, feedback, significance of tasks; Humphrey, Nahrgang, & Morgeson, 2007).

The final area in this knowledge domain is leadership. No topic studied by work and organizational psychologists has been as consistently as important to businesses and organizations as leadership and what makes leaders effective and ineffective.

It is an area of research and theory that is constantly evolving. Some research considers the traits of leaders, and the personality dimensions that tend to predict leader emergence and effectiveness (Judge, Bono, Ilies, & Gerhardt, 2002). A separate stream considers leadership style (distinguishing task- and person-oriented styles and their interaction). Contingency theories of leadership then expand research on leadership style to consider the situations and contexts in which different styles are effective. A third stream of research considers interpersonal aspects of leadership, for example, the interaction and exchanges of leaders and their staff, and how they influence performance at individual, team and organizational levels.

At the team level, psychologists have examined how teams are composed, and the processes that determine how they work most effectively (see e.g. West, 2012). Work on social psychology and group processes is a critical foundation of some of this research.

Knowledge Taster Box 3.4 Gender and leadership

The subject of women in leadership has attracted renewed research and some advances in in recent years. A frequently cited metaphor for the barriers preventing women progressing into leadership positions is the glass ceiling; an invisible barrier hindering promotion of women to higher management. However, it appears that the social psychology of women in leadership is much more complex that this simple metaphor. Researchers have argued that although women are beginning to break through the glass ceiling, their performance once promoted is placed under close scrutiny (Ryan & Haslam, 2007). Moreover, there emerge some fascinating findings about the contexts under which women are typically perceived as desirable leaders, and indeed appointed to leadership roles. Examining the performance of the UK FTSE 100 companies, research studies found archival evidence that women were more likely to be appointed to boards at time of organizational crisis, and especially so when share prices had fallen over successive months. Those organizations that did appoint women in these circumstances tended to perform better in the months that followed. This effect has been termed the glass cliff – the appointing of women to precarious positions of leadership at times of crisis.

The work has been developed further in experiments that showed that women were perceived as more effective (i.e. ideal) leaders for companies in situations of crisis (confirming the Think-Crisis-Think-Female bias). However, studies also showed that this applied specifically when the leader was expected to a) stay in the background and endure the crisis, or b) take responsibility for the company failure, or c) manage people and personnel issues through the crisis. There was not female bias if the leader was expected to d) act as a spokesperson, or e) take control and improve performance. This research uncovers some troubling trends for perceptions around women in leadership, strengthening the case for the glass cliff hypothesis. Although more women may be breaking into top leadership, the social psychological forces associated with their appointment may mean that they are essentially set up to lead in situations in which they have a much higher probability of failure than is typically experienced by their male counterparts.

Work design, organizational change and development

This knowledge domain represents the macro perspective on Occupational Psychology, and incorporates research into their cultures, climates, structures, strategies and physical environments. Research in this domain examines the backdrop for much that we have described from the field already.

The physical environments that people work in are the subject of research into human factors and ergonomics. On one hand, work in this area is concerned with how people interact with aspects of their workspace and environment (e.g. designing interfaces around users). On the other hand, when these ideas are scaled up to whole organizations, it is possible to consider how workspaces can be designed to be safer (by minimizing risks, and managing errors), and more healthy.

Then there is the psychological environment. When you walk into any business or organization, it's possible to feel the culture of it. Do people smile at you when they greet you? Do they appear to get on with each other? Does the work environment look cared for? How is the workspace arranged or decorated? How are people dressed?

All of these are clues about the accepted ways of working and doing business in the organization. Psychologists are interested in how cultures are created in organizations, how they are maintained, communicated and changed. At a more local level for staff in an organization, psychologists are interested in the so-called climate of teams and business units. Climates are concerned with what it feels like to work in particular part of the business, and they are generally concerned with some specific aspect or activity (e.g. climate for diversity, or climate for innovation).

At the top of organizations, in top management teams, psychologists are interested to learn how decisions are made, and how strategies are formed and implemented. For example, what is the impact on emotional reactions of top managers on the ways in which strategies are developed?

Finally, focusing still on the organization itself, occupational psychology is concerned with how they change and develop. Why does change succeed or fail in different situations? Organizational change is usually rooted in individual behaviour change, an area where psychologists are able to contribute well. Behaviour change strategies can be implemented through managing reward and incentives, individual learning and development, and diagnostics of systemic and organizational level enablers and barriers to change (e.g. team conflicts, procedures or communication lines in an organization).

Looking outside the organization, we can consider the cultural context that it operates in, and the challenges that come with making businesses effective when they operate globally across cultural and national borders. Global managers need new kinds of skills and abilities such as intercultural competence.

Knowledge Taster Box 3.5 Diversity climates

When managed in the right way, there are obvious potential benefits of a diverse workforce. Research in the area shows that diversity enhances performance when the tasks on which teams are working are complex and therefore require diverse perspectives in problem solving. Research also shows however, that diversity can lead to conflict where teams are set up and managed in a way that promotes formation of sub-groups of employees (e.g. men/women; older/younger workers; groups from different ethnic backgrounds).

Climate for diversity represents staff perceptions of the organization's values around having a diverse workforce. Research in work and organizational psychology shows that when people feel that their organization has a climate that values diversity because of the benefits it brings for knowledge and problem solving, there is a positive impact of diversity on performance. By contrast, when staff perceive that climate is such that diversity is only promoted to gain access to niche markets or avoid litigation, then there is no positive association between diversity and organization effectiveness (Gonzalez & Denisi, 2009).

This is helpful information for leaders and managers because they are able to have some impact on climate by developing pro-diversity policies and strategies, and communicating them effectively to staff.

Applying Psychology to work and organizations

This area of the foundations of Occupational Psychology is aligned to the practice skills of the profession. The knowledge areas we reviewed so far represent some of the key scientific pillars of the field. Occupational Psychologists are applied psychologists though and that means that they need to put the science to work, or apply it in practice.

The application of evidence in practice is referred to as the scientist-practitioner model, and is the way in which Occupational Psychologists go about their work.

Within the scientist-practitioner model, there are some specific practice skills that Occupational Psychologists learn about and some underpinning frameworks that guide the application of skills. Some example skills are:

- Interview techniques: methods of effectively designing interviews to understand experiences at work.
- Focus groups: working with groups of people to understand their experiences of work or to seek information on specific topics.
- Questionnaire design: constructing robust surveys and questionnaires to collect information from respondents.
- Facilitation skills: working with teams to implement projects and interventions.
- Giving feedback: providing feedback from assessments or performance evaluations, or on career progression, for example.
- Interpreting research and data: making decisions on the basis of research information already published or collected in an organization.
- Writing for different audiences: writing for organizational clients who might not be psychologists, including proposals, and reports of findings, presenting information in an understandable way.
- Project management: being accountable for delivery of projects to clients, and ensuring that projects are effectively planned and executed.

A guiding framework for applying the scientist-practitioner model in work with organizational clients is the consultancy cycle (see later in this Chapter). At the heart of this framework is an evidence-based approach to problem solving.

The final element in this domain is ethics. Occupational Psychologists are committed to acting according the ethical standards of the British Psychological Society. This is a significant strength of the profession of Occupational Psychology, which when combined with the regulation of psychologists by the Health and Care Professions Council, provides assurance of the professional ethical standards and integrity of qualified practitioners.

Research design, advanced data-gathering and analytical techniques

And so we come to the final knowledge area of Occupational Psychology: research methodology. It is the foundation of the profession, and the means by which all of the areas, theories and research findings we have highlighted in this brief tour have been accumulated. Research methodology is certainly not the sexiest of the core knowledge areas of Occupational Psychology, but it is the one that gives the profession distinctiveness, and real value in practice. It is where core technical skills of the profession reside.

If you are psychology undergraduate student, or encountering psychology for the first time in your secondary education, or in a different bachelors programme, then you should be familiar with the basics of research methodology. Research from a positivist paradigm follows the scientific method, in terms of using theory to generate testable hypotheses that are investigated in lab or field studies, usually utilizing quantitative data. Often, theory building is informed by qualitative data describing and elaborating people's experiences of work.

As you become a specialist in Occupational Psychology however, you can expect that your understanding of research will be stepped up to a more advanced level; it will be demanding. Yet, the basic process of research is the same:

Research design: planning research protocols that will effectively test hypotheses and therefore elaborate theoretical propositions. Typically research in psychology is concerned with researching how variables co-vary (a correlational design; e.g. testing the correlation of personality traits with job performance) or how controlled manipulation of variables affect outcomes (an experimental design; e.g. comparing performance change for a group attending training at work with a control group who have not received training).

In the case of experimental designs, most fieldwork would be considered quasi-experimental because organizations are not lab settings and it is therefore difficult to control conditions under which interventions are carried out. In this sense they are not truly "controlled".

In advanced methodology, researchers are also interested to test *when* significant effects (correlations or experimental effects) are observed, and do so using moderation designs. They are also concerned with testing *why* effects are observed, testing this through mediation designs. To be theoretically robust, these kinds of research designs require longitudinal data collection (data collected over several points in time).

Data-gathering techniques are concerned with compiling information that will be subjected to analyses. Data might be quantitative or qualitative (text-based).

Data analysis involves scrutinizing and testing data either through inferential quantitative tests, or qualitative exploration through content analysis and more advanced techniques such as thematic analysis. In the case of quantitative analyses, there are a number of advanced techniques to learn about (e.g. regression analysis, structural equation modelling, factor analysis), many of which are developed by researchers in psychology, and in Occupational Psychology specifically.

From a constructivist perspective, research is about understanding how the "reality" of organizational life is constructed by social structures, cultural and historical contexts, and language (the way we speak about work and organizations).

We want to emphasize again, the value of knowing about research methodology and how do conduct (and consume) good science. The technical skills you learn as an Occupational Psychologist are rare in businesses and organizations. That means they are extremely valuable. If you master research, you will have a strong and unique skillset with which to build your career as an Occupational Psychologist.

Plus, research in real organizations is fascinating and powerful (see the Knowledge Taster Box).

Knowledge Taster Box 3.6 When Human Resource Management is life or death

A research article published in 2006 in the Journal of Organizational Behaviour reported a remarkable finding about Human Resource Management (HRM). The study (West, Guthrie, Dawson, Borrill, & Carter, 2006) examined the relationship between the use of particular HR practices in hospitals in the UK, and patient mortality. The study reported that even after controlling for common predictors of mortality in hospitals (e.g. doctors per number of beds, GPs per 100,000 population in the local area), the use of high performance HR systems was associated with lower mortality in hospitals. In hospitals where effective HR systems were implemented, fewer patients died.

This is a good example of a valuable piece of information about organizations and their management that has real consequences for people's lives, and that could only be established through sound scientific research. How did the researchers arrive at this finding?

The importance of sound methodology in this example shows how research can be effectively put to work to understand real and critical outcomes.

The values of Occupational Psychologists

There are four key themes in this section. We first look at the subject of values – both professional and personal – and how these should impact the work of occupational psychologists. We then go on to look at the equally interesting topic of business ethics: what are mean and how they are demonstrated in the workplace. Then we look at the consultancy cycle and, in particular, how our values may be compromised by the way we carry out our work. Finally, we discuss evidence-based management which, when properly applied, should help occupational psychologists to work in ways that both meet organizational and business demands, whilst, at the same time, allowing practitioners to maintain their professional and personal integrity.

Values

We learn our values at an early age. The values help us to determine what is good and bad in life; what is acceptable and unacceptable; what is honest and dishonest. Parents pass on their values to their children, and society provides messages and cues, both obvious and subtle, about how we are expected to conduct ourselves in our daily lives.

Geert Hofstede's pioneering work demonstrates how values not only are learned early in our lives but that they can also differ from culture to another.

Values then are statements about how we should conduct ourselves. They provide a way of enabling us to make judgements at work, but they are also judgemental – they are not neutral, they provide the criteria by which we assess our conduct and not just our outcomes. For example, let's take one outcome which we would all like to achieve: having a satisfied client. But if the outcome is achieved by misrepresenting data, or only presenting results the client would like to hear, then clearly professional values will have been violated.

Professional values

The British Psychological Society's Code of Ethics and Conduct (2018) addresses key ethical issues for psychological practice.

The key areas of ethical concern for psychologists include:

- **Multiple relationships** – where the psychologist owes an allegiance to several different stakeholders.
- **Personal relationships** – where the psychologist misjudges or violates the trust of a client or clients.
- **Unclear or inadequate standards of practice** – where the psychologist is unaware of, or disregards, the current systems in use by peers or others in similar work
- **Breaches of confidentiality** where rules and constraints were broken or not clarified in advance with stakeholders.
- **Competencies** – where excessive or misleading claims are made or where inadequate safeguards and monitoring exist for new areas of work.
- **Research issues** – including falsifying data, failing to obtain consent, plagiarism or failing to acknowledge another's contribution.
- **Health problems** affecting performance or conduct.
- **Bringing the profession or the Society in to disrepute.**

(p6/7)

The code also goes on to state that some of the entries listed above include "lack of information, poor planning or carelessness. Reflective practice, peer support and transparency of professional activity would prevent problems occurring or developing into serious concerns" (p7).

Some, maybe many, ethical dilemmas could be resolved, and possibly would be prevented in the first place, by the professional conduct of psychologists.

Whilst the code does not talk of values, it does list four ethical principles:

Respect – "value the dignity and worth of all persons, with sensitivity to the dynamics of perceived authority or influence over clients and with particular regard to peoples' rights, including those of privacy and self-determination"

(p10)

Competence – "value the continuing development and maintenance of high standards of competence in their professional work, and the importance of preserving their ability to function optimally within the recognized limits of their knowledge, skill, training, education and experience"

(p14)

Responsibility – "value their responsibilities to clients, to the general public and to the profession and science of Psychology, including the avoidance of harm and the prevention of misuse or abuse of their contribution to society"

(p18)

Integrity – "value honesty, accuracy, clarity and fairness in new interactions with all persons, and to seek to promote integrity in all facets of their scientific and professional endeavours"

(p21)

In fact, these principles are little different from those found in other professions such as accountancy, law and engineering. Rather than demonstrating a lack of imagination on the part of psychologists (which is always possible), it really shows how similar different professions are at their core. These values, or ethical statements are the same because the ethical concerns of all professions are essentially the same.

As most psychologists within the BPS work in clinical or educational settings, it probably makes sense that the descriptions of these principles is oriented toward this majority. These principles obviously apply equally well to occupational psychologists but need to be re-fashioned in terms of describing the expectations. We will attempt to do this, for two, in particular: respect and responsibility.

Respect: value the dignity and work of all persons. Whilst occupational psychologists will be seen as members of the professional and managerial cadre, and their immediate clients will be in management, they need to ensure that they look at the interests of all people in the organization and beyond.

Responsibility: value their responsibility to clients, to organizations, to the general public, to the profession and to the science of psychology. This means acting as an independent voice, where necessary, and to identify when and how psychology theory and research can influence organizational practice.

These principles are easy to write down but harder to practice. The work of an occupational psychologist often entails working in multidisciplinary teams and most often with individuals from Human Resources and Learning and Development departments.

In such teams, the value of having an occupational psychologist can be overlooked. OPs are most often asked to comment on specific technical issues, most significantly around the areas of recruitment, selection and assessment. The wider contributions OPs can make are often not considered primarily because people in other functions are not aware.

The client in such situations is invariably somebody from management. The need is often quite specific and urgent. It is not surprising to find in many instances that a preferred solution may even be implied. These pressures, subtle though they are, are undoubtedly felt on occasion and whilst they can be difficult to resist, it is important that OPs do not simply succumb to them.

In these circumstances, OPs will experience some tension and this will invariably be due to the conflict between personal, professional and organizational values.

When it comes to ethical decision-making there are three basic criteria to consider.

1 Utilitarianism – providing the greatest good to the greatest number of people.
2 Right – where individuals make decisions in line with the fundamental liberties as set out in legislation, for example.

3   Justice – that rules are imposed fairly and impartially so that people
    are treated equitably.

(Robbins, Judge, & Campbell, 2012)

In organizations, decision-making tends to fall into the utilitarianism
category. Decision makers are under pressure, they need quick answers
and action how to be taken swiftly. One common response, in our
experience involves looking at how other organizations have dealt with
the same or similar issue. This approach obviously has some merit and
the old adage "reinventing the wheel" is often brought up in such situations. So, if you are trying to come up with a better way of managing
performance why not look at what others have done and implement
that. Once a lot of organizations have used the same methodology and
implemented similar solutions, this will then be referred to as "best
practice". So now the approach is officially sanctioned and becomes
embedded as the best and most practical way forward. Any deviation
from this, therefore, clearly must be "less than best practice" or even
"bad practice". In fact, what has really been produced is not "best"
practice but "common" practice which are not the same thing at all.
Fads and fashions can become embedded and institutionalized, and
accepted as the right approach.

Psychologists have a critical role in examining the appropriateness
of such actions. Unfortunately some psychologists are too willing to
conform to the behavioural norms and expectations that exist with
organizations. In other words, they forget or park their personal and
professional values and make utilitarian decisions which are often based
on the need for a speedy response designed to improve productivity
and profitability or to promote a positive view of the organization.

The response of psychologist, when challenged, is often to say "I
have no choice. This is what my manager wants". Whilst we may empa-
thize with our colleagues, it is in precisely these situations where our
professional values are tested. It is our response on these occasions
which show whether we truly believe and adhere to these values or
not. We understand this is not easy, particularly for someone starting-
out in their career, but that is not a good reason for not behaving
professionally.

Part of the problem, when compared to other professions, like
medicine, engineering, law, accountancy – the skills and experience an

occupational psychologist brings are not necessarily called upon. Others may not be aware of what an OP has to offer or may simply believe that psychology is irrelevant. In these situations, psychologists:

(a) need to know the research and theories and
(b) be prepared to make their voice heard.

In this respect working as an OP within an organizations can be more difficult than one being brought in as an expert. In the latter case, the expertise and knowledge of the person has been acknowledged and will be listened to more.

Giving in to these pressures and demands may make life easier, but unfortunately it doesn't make you a psychologist.

Consultancy: internal and external

Occupational psychologists will, whether they have the term psychologist in their job title or not, often be working in a consultancy capacity, either internally or externally,

Having psychologist as part of your job title undoubtedly makes life easier. People will have a set of expectations (not necessarily all positive) about you, your role and your potential contribution.

The public sector still employs occupational psychologists and clearly values the expertise they provide. Government departments in the UK Civil Service which employ occupational psychologists include the Department for Work and Pensions, the Ministry of Defence and the Home Office. The work is varied, covering a range of areas including stress, well-being, performance management and assessment. In the private sector, from our experience, the numbers have declined and where they are used it is more likely to be involved in selection, assessment and talent management. In executive search firms it is the assessment expertise that is particularly valued, where psychologists not only bring thoroughness to the process but also lend some credibility to the firm itself.

Often within organizations, however, psychologists will be part of an HR team or a learning and development department. Job titles will not reflect the education and training of the person and, as a consequence, their expertise can be easily overlooked and even, on occasions, be seen as irrelevant. In these situations, to be accepted by their colleagues, individuals will, for understandable reasons, not see themselves as psychologists any longer. We often come across people working in organizations who will say "I did a Masters in Occupational Psychology, but I don't get a chance to practice this anymore". This is a pity in two ways:

First, for the individual, there was clearly an interest, possibly even a passion, for occupational psychology which motivated them to invest time, energy and money in obtaining the necessary qualification.

Second, for organizations, psychology has the potential to make the workplace better than it is, to improve well-being, to identify leaders, to reduce prejudice, to improve productivity – to name just a few areas. To leave that experience behind is to deny organizations of the positive benefits that the discipline can provide.

Our advice, if you find yourself in this situation, is to always remember that, despite what others think of you or how they might describe you, always remember you are a psychologist, and that you have, as a consequence, access to knowledge and expertise that will be different to others and a perspective on an organization's problem that others will not have. These are the aspects of our work that make us different from other disciplines and where psychologists have the greatest value to add.

Psychologists who come into organizations to provide consultancy, support and advice naturally start with an advantage over those working within organizations do not have – namely that they are already perceived as being experts in their chosen specialism – otherwise what is the point of bringing them in? The expectations, therefore, are likely to be different: people within the organizations will be asking for your thoughts, opinions and insights. All of these will be based upon your interpretation of the current theories and research.

It is these perspectives and insights, based upon a thorough grounding of the psychology literature that enhances your credibility as a psychologist. A small point but a crucial one: you may be providing consultancy services (both as internal employee or as someone brought into the organizations) but you are not a consultant. One of the objectives in founding Pearn Kandola was to have occupational psychology seen as a profession in its own right. The practice was built by looking at how other professions conducted themselves e.g. lawyers, architects, accountants, engineers. None of them described themselves as consultants. There is of course nothing wrong with being a consultant and nor can you stop the way other people describe you. Nevertheless, we can control the way we describe ourselves. To not describe ourselves as psychologists is to deny not just of our education and training but part of our identity.

The consultancy cycle

It is a fascinating aspect about books on occupational psychology that whilst all of them describe the theoretical underpinning of our work, few, if any, describe how to work in a consultancy capacity. Having knowledge and expertise are clearly essential pre-requisites to being an effective, if not outstanding, occupational psychologist. Being able to apply this in messy organizational settings means having to have an understanding of the process of consultancy.

In this regard, experience undoubtedly helps. The practical problems of running a project as well as the ethical dilemmas that arise become easier to deal with once you have had several projects or assignments under your belt, as long as, of course, you reflect on your experience.

The consultancy cycle provide a readily available way of managing yourself and your clients during an assignment. A most useful, and the most relevant for occupational psychologists, document is that from the BPS which describes the assessment guidelines for chartership as an occupational psychologist. The document is clear and transparent – anyone involved in going through the supervised practice process can access it. For our purposes it provides the essential information you need to understand what the consultancy cycle is and how it is applicable to occupational psychologists. There are several steps to the consultancy cycle (see Table 3.1 and Figure 3.1):

- Establishing agreements with customers
- Identifying needs and problems
- Formulating solutions
- Implementing and reviewing solutions
- Evaluating outcomes
- Reporting and reflecting on outcomes

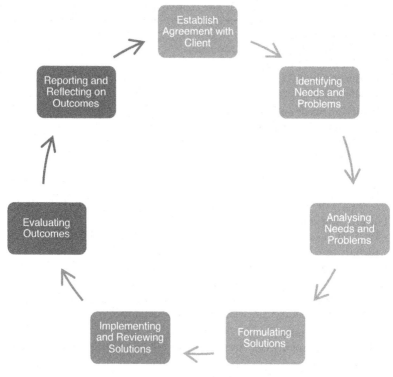

Figure 3.1 Consultancy cycle

Establishing agreements with customers

This first stage is to clarify roles, responsibilities and outcomes. What is expected by the client in this situation and for this project? What will the client commit to doing? What are the boundaries for the responsibilities i.e. who will do what?

In many respects this can been seen as clarification in the contractual sense: the obligations of all parties involved and what the expected outputs are.

At this stage too the timelines will need to established so everyone knows when the project will be completed and what the expected output will be e.g. a report, a presentation, a workshop.

Table 3.1 The consultancy cycle

Establishing agreement
– Agreement of the role of the psychologist
– Responsibility of the psychologist
– Clarity of objectives
– Establish timeframes

Identifying needs and problems
– Establishing the actual needs and problems
– Probing and testing assumptions about the actual issues
– Re-defining objectives if necessary

Analyzing needs and problems
– Analyzing the data obtained
– Using psychological research and theory to help explain what is observed.

Formulating solutions
– Formulating solutions based on psychological research and theory
– Identifying relevant aspects of the psychological literature to inform
  solutions that are arrived at

Implementing & reviewing solutions
– Establishing available options, and implementing a chosen solution
– Anticipating risks and reviewing progress of solutions

Evaluating outcomes
– How did the project/assignment meet the objectives established at the start
  of the project?

Reporting and reflecting on outcomes
– Reflecting on the project/assignment
– What went well?
– What obstacles were encountered?

Next time
– What ethical issues were raised and how well were they dealt with?
– What would you do differently?

Identifying needs and problems

In many instances the client (by this we mean the person or people commissioning the piece of work) will have a clear idea of what the problem is and how they believe having a psychologist would help them.

It is **always** important for a psychologist to understand the background to any potential assignment and how the client has reached the conclusion that this is the piece of work that is required to provide a solution. Usually, the issues will be straightforward e.g. develop a new selection process for a particular role or set of roles. On other occasions the origins of the project and its proposed solutions will be altogether more ambiguous. E.g. creating a gender network in order to increase the amount of women in senior leadership roles.

In these cases (both real incidentally) however, the assumptions and approaches need to be questioned and clarified and any assumptions, gently but firmly, challenged. For example, the client might insist that they wanted to improve their graduate recruitment process by targeting Oxford and Cambridge students only. In this case, the psychologist would need to question the efficacy of such an approach as much talent would be ignored. There would be diversity implications too if this approach was adopted.

In the second case, the client may be very clear that a gender network is necessary to improve the representation of women at senior levels. The client may well be aware that their competitors in the same sector had implemented such an initiative. Then the psychologist would need to test their assumptions and challenge their view on how this would indeed assist the organization in achieving its objectives.

In both cases, there is a responsibility on the psychologist not only to understand the nature of the work, but to test assumptions using psychological research as a basis for the questions.

Failing to do this, will undermine the rest of the project and ultimately reduce the possibility of a successful outcome and positive evaluation.

Analysing needs and problems

At this stage the psychologist will need to know what tools will be needed to analyse the problems. Carrying out a well-being audit in an organization for example could be done by using quantitative and/or qualitative data. A survey could be sent to employees which will provide an indication of issues on a range of pre-defined and pre-determined factors. The breadth of information obtained from a wide range of people will help to make up for the potential lack of sensitivity that any survey, whatever the topic, can provide.

Qualitative data e.g. from focus groups and interviews, will enable specific issue to be identified from that organization but these we know are time intensive and relatively expensive for clients to carry out. Comparison with other organizations is also not directly possible with such an approach.

Whatever tools and approaches you decide to use needs to be considered carefully. Sometimes it can be quite obvious, given what a client says, how something should be addressed. On other occasions more thought needs to be given.

It is important that psychologists understand the potential range of data analysis and data-gathering methods that are available. Choosing a method also means rejecting others. Are you clear why you have rejected the other possible approaches?

This pre-supposes of course that the psychologist knows of other methodologies, which in turn means keeping ourselves up to date.

The data then needs to be analysed, the objectives of the project together with the underlying research framework you are using will help guide analysis. The way to evaluate and analyse the data should have been clear from the outset. Typically, a combination of methods will be used so you need to be clear about how this will be analysed to provide a coherent picture of what is going on with the issue being examined.

There may be contradictions and ambiguities in the data, which may or may not be important, but they do need to be explored.

Formulating solutions

In many respects it is this that client is most interested in. A coherent set of actions with a plan of some sort attached is what a client wants. It will not be enough just to present results. There was an occasion when one of the actions was working with a group of occupational psychologists. They described their approach as one of facilitation: they provided the method, collected the data and provided the analysis. They did not feel it was their role to provide recommendations; instead they facilitated in discussions to provide the actions. An approach that is client centred and empowering. In the next the breath, however, they also said they could not believe how poor the actions were! This is not facilitation, it is failing to take responsibility. There is nothing wrong with a facilitative approach, but it can lead to the accusation that psychologists have little to offer. To use an old joke – a consultant is someone who borrows your watch to tell you the time – and then steals the watch. In this particular case the dismissive attitude toward the clients actions demonstrated that the psychologists know what "good" looked like. Having the confidence to put forward your own views is a critical part of the role. Again, this is founded upon a deep understanding of our chosen field of expertise.

There will be areas where you are more confident about the recommendations than others. When presenting back to the client, start with these and then share your areas of doubt. Being transparent with the client not only enhances trust but also enhances your competence.

Knowing the literature is important as you need to have an understanding about what has proven to work and just as critically what has not worked.

Competitors' actions and benchmarking practice can form part of your evaluations of actions to take, but be open-minded about whether these have been properly evaluated.

Your role in the project is that of a psychologist, to provide a particular perspective on the problems and issues being examined. This will of necessity, if you are doing your job properly, mean putting forward ideas and challenging others' based on psychological theories and research. Do not negate and undermine your role and undermine the profession by not applying psychology thoroughly and thoughtfully.

Implementing and reviewing solutions

A psychologist from an external consultancy may find they have a limited role here, but this depends on the solutions provided.

Internal psychologists will, more often than not, be involved in the implementation recommended actions. There will be pressure to find cheaper and quicker solutions, which is not necessarily a bad thing. However, the client needs to understand the risks involved with doing this. In addition, you need to be clear about areas where you cannot make any compromises.

Ideally, some sort of review process will be involved to monitor progress of implementation, so a plan or roadmap is very helpful.

Evaluating outcomes

The guidelines recognize the potential problems where "sometimes a client will not pay for an evaluation" however it does go on to say "but you can evaluate whether the outcomes agreed with the customer have been met and explain how you have evaluated this".

You should be prepared on occasion to conduct an evaluation of your work at your own cost. This may seem an unnecessary thing to do, but if a client is unwilling to pay for an evaluation, then on occasion, we must do that ourselves.

If the evaluation is to be done independently the results are likely to be more objective. In any event we need to be honest about outcomes with the client and with ourselves if our work as psychologists is to develop and improve.

Reporting and reflecting on outcomes

Some sort of project review process is helpful and necessary.

Feedback needs to be obtained from the client about how they felt about the project, the levels of expertise provided and the outcomes.

The teams need to share their own reflections about how they felt about the project. In practice, this tends to happen for larger projects, but certainly ethical dilemmas may need to be discussed within the team and beyond so that the experiences are shared, understood and applied in future projects.

Evidence Based Management

Occupational Psychologists are *scientist-practitioners* and therefore apply scientific evidence to their practice as psychologists in organizations. How does this work in reality? A practical tool to illustrate, which is close allied to OP is Evidence Based Management (EBM). This has been defined by one of the leading experts in the field, Denise Rousseau as "*translating principles based on best evidence into organizational practices*"

In her paper, actually her presidential speech to the Academy of Management, Rousseau stated that many people, and certainly MBA students have never worked for a great manager not for a great organization. Too many decisions, even from people who have been trained at management schools, are based on "personal experience to the exclusion of more systematic knowledge" (Rousseau, 2006, p227).

Yet, it is ironic, isn't it, that whenever our personal perspective of a problem is challenged one of the first questions we will ask is "What is your evidence for that?" In other words, we need evidence to show that our experiences may not provide us with the best solutions and yet feel less inclined to provide evidence to back-up our own experiences

And yet as Rousseau continues, many people want to be great managers. The motivation exists to do things differently, even though in practice we continue with our age-old ways of dealing with issues.

A crucial element in EBM, it seems to us is highlighted in Rousseau's presidential address: namely that of best evidence. "Best practice" and "Best evidence" may be the same, but they could also be different and the psychologists role is to seek "best evidence". This can be done in a number of ways but it involves examining a complete range of studies on any given topic. It can be all too easy to look only at research and other findings that support your point of view so we need to see alternative points of view, which challenge our own. This involves not just looking at academic papers, but also what is referred to as the "grey literature" e.g. unpublished papers and conference papers. Our own professional experience and observations also play a part but we have to be transparent in representing them as such so that we all, clients included, can determine how relevant each piece of research is.

An EBM based process will look like this therefore:

1   The problem – the manager or practitioner problem, question or issue
2   Gather internal organizational evidence or data, which will lead to a possible restatement of the problem
3   Gather external evidence – published research and systematic reviews
4   View of stakeholders and those likely be affected by the decisions.
5   Analyse, appraise and make decisions that attempt to integrate those sources of information.

In many ways these reflect the consultancy process described earlier. The key difference, it appears to be is conducting the systematic reviews. This will not be possible within the timescales for every project you undertake. However, within your chosen speciality in the field of occupational psychology it is an activity that can, and needs, to be carried out on a regular basis. It is not just about keeping ourselves updated but being prepared to have our views challenged by the evidence. It is through these mechanisms that we develop and properly represent the potential that psychology has to improve organizations and peoples' lives.

As eminent psychologist Kurt Lewin once said, "There is nothing as practical as a good theory".

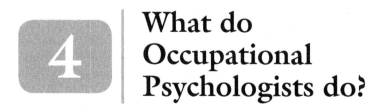

What do Occupational Psychologists do?

In this book so far, we have focused on what on the knowledge base for Occupational Psychology and the general approaches and values that Occupational Psychologists take to their work. In this Chapter, we answer a key question that you are likely to have, having read this far – *what do Occupational Psychologists do?* We mean here, what are the key jobs, activities, practice areas and tasks that OPs work on day-to-day and through their careers. The objective of this Chapter is to provide an overview and some examples, in the key areas of practice of OPs.

Assessment at work

Psychological assessment is core business for Occupational Psychology practitioners. With such a wealth of relevant theory and technical capability in the field, this is an area where psychologists contribute real value to organizational practice. There a number of ways in which this contribution is made. One way is through practice as specialist assessment consultancy. Test publishers (organizations that design, research and sell test products to business clients) are among the biggest group of employers of new Occupational Psychologists and are generally highly innovative too. Their work is to apply advances in assessment technology and develop assessment and analytical techniques that make assessment at work more effective.

However, in this area of practice, psychologists do not work solely in specialist consultancies. Many practice within organizations as specialists and work with Human Resources, or other within-organization clients on technical aspects of assessment. This might be applied to recruitment and selection, or performance management practice predominantly, or in other areas of management too. Work in this vein could be either advisory or hands-on. So on one hand, you might work with senior managers and others to advise on assessment process and strategy. On the other hand, you could be hands on running interviews with candidates, or assessment centre processes, or working with test data, or evaluating job applications. There is a vast array of work available.

Work in the advisory capacity draws heavily on knowledge and technical specialism. Many of the core theories of work and organizational psychology are shared with education in human resources management (HRM) and general management, so it is safe to assume that clients have some awareness and understanding of the principles of motivation, social psychology and even some aspects of research methodology, for example. Where insight is sought is generally on specific advanced issues of evaluating or improving the effectiveness of assessment at work. This general theme encompasses a variety of issues.

Very commonly, the role involves appraisal of evidence to support the reliability, validity and fairness of assessment processes and techniques. This evidence can be pre-existing (i.e. have been collected by the client, or supplied by a third party) or might involve primary data collection. Either way, research skills and understanding are needed. Clients are looking almost exclusively for clarity about the questions they have about assessment effectiveness, and it is therefore critical that you are able to understand the evidence and articulate the implications clearly. In the past, I have been presented with portfolios of evidence, for which the client is seeking some independent advice. The quality and presentation of the evidence is variable, and is usually (although not always) wrapped up with varying degrees of positive spin, either to support sales, or represent a position. The analytic problem solving involved in making sense of it though is fascinating, stretching and consequently very rewarding.

Psychologists also conduct primary research on assessment effectiveness. In selection, this could mean for example, evaluating the validity of a psychometric test locally in an organization. For these kinds of activity, understanding the assessment of psychological characteristics and the assessment of performance criteria are equally important. Psychologists can evaluate not only the validity of a selection assessment, but also the quality of the criteria used in any evaluation research. The job is to be critical, and robust in terms of the research undertaken. Similar validation questions might be addressed concerning assessment centres or interviews. Here the advice being sought is how to make evidence-based improvements. Again, a critical approach is paramount. The role of the technical expert is not one of endorsement, but instead of interpretation; that is, interpretation of the evidence to make a justifiable, defensible and practical recommendation of how practice can be improved or changed.

Rising beyond providing technical advice, psychologists might also be called upon for strategic advice about assessment. For example, suppose that an organization has developed a new set of corporate values or competencies, and wants to ensure that they are reflected in people's behaviour. How can this be done? One means is through assessment. By embedding the values and competencies in assessment criteria to be applied at selection, and performance management, positive value- and competency-relevant behaviour is selected into the organization and promoted amongst existing employees. The deployment and management of such a strategic development could be led by a psychologist.

On the implementation side of assessment, psychologists are involved in the practicalities of assessing job candidates, employees and others in the workplace. The role of the psychologist on an assessment team is different between projects. Psychologists might be brought in to lead a specific part of an assessment. For example, perhaps a client would like psychometric testing to be incorporated into an assessment centre. A psychologist could be delegated the task of managing the integration, and conducting the assessments.

Psychologists could be part of multidisciplinary teams of assessment practitioners, working with general managers and HR professionals. In such cases, the psychologist is employed to carry out assessments (e.g. in interviews) alongside these other professionals, and it is likely that they also provide a unique perspective that complements the rest of the team.

Alternatively, assessments could be undertaken by psychologist-only teams. In a consultancy approach, teams of psychologists might assume responsibility for managing assessment at various levels. External consultants are generally brought in to provide specialist assessment services such as assessment centres. Internally, teams of psychologists might manage key strategic assessment systems such as graduate recruitment. Examples where teams of psychologists work on such projects include the UK Civil Service, the Police Services, and in Shell.

Skills needed for practice of assessment at work

The skills needed for this practice area depend very much on what approach the psychologists is taking. If working in an advisory capacity, then technical, analytical, problem solving, critical interpretive and communication skills are all essential. If methodology is not your strength, then this aspect of practice isn't either. Critical thinking is also crucial. You must be able to critique, identify strengths and limitations, and question evidence.

On the implementation side, the skills needed are team-working, communication, time management, planning and organization, listening and observation. To be an effective assessor, you must be able to work with others, listen and observe objectively and critically, and manage your natural biases. You must also be committed to working to meet project deadlines, and be organized with your own tasks, workload and time.

Learning, development and performance management

After much consideration about how to divide the practice domains of learning, training, performance management, coaching and career development, we decided not to. This is more than just a conceptual convenience. Rather, we believe that these areas are very difficult to separate from a systems perspective. Activity undertaken in any of these domains generally has some effect on another, or indeed may be a result of, or in the service of another. In short, psychologists that work in any of the following areas, are almost certainly making contributions directly or indirectly to the others:

- Training and Development at Work
- Performance Assessment and Management

- Coaching
- Career Development

At the core of all of these practice areas is the theme of individual development at work. The linkages should be clear. The purpose of development at work is twofold: 1) to help people improve performance or learn new skills needed to improve organizational performance; 2) to help people progress and develop in their careers. Training and learning is generally therefore linked to some determination of development that is needed for people, provided through performance management or career development practice. Coaching is a relational form of development that complements other forms of training and learning interventions. As a practitioner, this awareness is important so that you understand how your work makes an impact on different aspects of people management. We will discuss each area under a separate subheading, but we underline that we consider them inextricably linked.

Performance assessment and management

We have talked in the previous section about practice of assessment at work. Much of the technical specialism applied in assessment of people for selection is similarly applied in the assessment of people in terms of their job performance. Techniques of assessment tool design, statistical analysis, competency assessment and so forth, are central to ensuring that performance is assessed at work fairly and thoroughly. The contribution of the psychologist to performance measurement should similarly be critical and questioning.

Keep in mind that a core expertise of psychologists is understanding behaviour, and from our disciplinary perspective, all performance is behaviour. Results at work (sales volume, outputs etc.) are one metric that indicates individual performance, but they reflect only the outcomes or ends of performance, not the *means* or *process* of performance. Moreover, performance outcomes are often influenced by factors other than individual capability (e.g. market environment, product features, team context), and so a results-based view of performance is necessarily limited. Taking the argument further, let's assume that a person's results at work are weak. What can be done to improve that performance? It would be impossible to say with any certainty unless we understand *why* performance is weak, or put another way, what a person is doing that is contributing to poor performance, and alongside, what a person is doing well, or positively. Taking this together, psychologists' contribution to practice in performance assessment and management has a strong emphasis on defining, explaining and elaborating performance behaviour, and operationalizing it in some form that can be measured effectively. The emergence of the competency approach to performance assessment is an excellent example of this in practice. Other literature worth exploring is around 360-degree or multi-source approaches to assessment of performance. In these approaches, performance is assessed by not only line managers, but also colleagues subordinates and even customers.

As with recruitment and selection assessment, the practice undertaken by work and organizational psychologists could be advisory or hands-on implementation. You might be involved in technical development or evaluation of performance measurement, or involved in the practical tasks of evaluating employee performance.

Performance management is obviously more than just measurement though. So what comes next? There are two main steps: feedback and intervention. Interventions to improve or develop performance are dealt with below through training, development and coaching. A note on feedback is worthwhile here.

In 1996, a paper in Psychological Bulletin by Kluger and DeNisi (1996) shattered a cornerstone of management practice. Conventional management wisdom had held that performance feedback was essential for performance management, and always positive. The research undertaken by Kluger and DeNisi however, found that in 600 published studies, one third of them reported that feedback resulted in performance decreases: in a third of cases, giving feedback was detrimental to performance. Subsequent research has examined why this is the case, highlighting issues of source credibility, feedback content, and organizational context as relevant for affecting the impact of feedback.

For psychologists, one-to-one discussion, interaction, reflection and feedback are core skills in respect of wider psychological interventions such as counselling and therapy for example. Practice in this area could involve providing performance feedback to employees, or leaders about their performance, and ensuring that the content is accurate, appropriately communicated, clear and solution-focused in terms of exploring how to act on the feedback. Remaining evidence-based, non-judgmental and supportive are key qualities that psychologists can bring to practice in this area.

Training and development at work

The training and development work undertaken by work and organizational psychologists may be organized into a loosely defined set of subdomains. These help to highlight the various areas you might work in.

The first might be termed *prescribed development*, and follows logically from performance assessment. Having identified development needs from performance measurement at work, this kind of training activity involves specifying relevant training and development activity that will enable skills gaps to be closed. The role of the psychologist here is to determine the more effective and practical learning activity for the specific development need. For example, perhaps formal training is required if skills gaps are acute. Alternatively, on-job developmental assignments might be more appropriate, and a key role of the psychologist is to identify appropriate tasks, projects and activities to promote skills development and learning.

For some areas of work skills and competencies, psychologists may be in the best position to actually deliver learning interventions. For example, in areas of interpersonal skills such as negotiation and influencing, social psychology is a key foundation, and so psychologists are well placed to design appropriate programmes of learning and development. The delivery of training and learning by psychologists could be divided into both general and specialist forms.

General development programmes are those that apply across multiple sectors and organizations. Leadership development programmes are the most common and are designed to help people develop skills for the transition to leadership, or moving to more senior leadership roles. Leader development is a core area of business for practitioners and the content such programmes includes some basic theories of organizational behaviour, change management and usually performance management. The quality of programmes is variable, which means that their impact is also variable. In our view, developing general programmes of development is underselling what we do as psychologists. The basic leadership development programme can be designed and delivered by any MBA qualified consultant, and psychologists can and need to do better than this in order to differentiate and ensure value in our offering.

This differentiation can be applied in two ways. One, through pro-gramme customization. The analytical skill of psychologists enable profiling of organizational needs and cultures in a more precise way to determine learning needs. Thinking back to the notion of training transfer, psychologists could use this analysis to tailor learning interven-tions to these specific needs, and to promote training transfer. Delivery of greater return on investment of training as a consequence would be attractive to clients.

The second area of training delivery by psychologists that is even more valuable, is the sharing and dissemination of knowledge and skills of occupational psychology. You might argue that effectively up-skilling clients such that they are able to perform work of psychologists has the potential to take work away from us ultimately, or even has ethical risks because non-psychologists lack foundation understanding needed for complex practice of psychology. Both are legitimate concerns, but most likely unwarranted.

In the case of ethical risk, it is important to keep in perspective the knowledge and skills that could be shared or disseminated. Procedural skills that are straightforward to apply and which are backed up by strong evidence carry no risk at all in our view. For example, research shows us the value of using structured interviewing, a process which is also ethically more sound than unstructured interviews (which are prone to bias). Managers and others could learn how to add structure to interviews quite easily, and apply it in their day to day practice. Simi-larly in the case of goal setting, the practice of setting better objectives for staff and understanding the process by which they are delivered is not complicated to apply if it is set out effectively in learning activity.

Sharing evidence-based perspectives that are straightforward or pro-cedural in psychology, yet more advanced and detailed than could be delivered by other non-psychologist consultants is key to differentiat-ing what psychologists do, and achieving impact from the research and knowledge that psychologists have accumulated. In this respect, far from taking work away from the profession, skills sharing arguably is essential in showing the value of our contribution. There will always be specialist advanced contributions that psychologists will be able to make to build on procedural applications. Advanced knowledge arguably has more value too, as it is more unique (a point we return to later).

As a case in point, look at the success of the BPS psychological testing centre, which accredits training for psychologists and non-psychologists in psychometric testing. The competencies of testing are set out clearly and procedurally. The BPS audits and quality controls training programmes through verification of approved assessors. Those assessors are then able to train practitioners how to use psychological testing effectively and ethically. It is a massive area of business for psychologists that not only supports training businesses, but also enables assessment business for the profession.

Training evaluation

How do you evaluate the return-on-investment or impact of training and learning at work? We propose that occupational psychologists are the key experts to answer this question. No other profession has the combination of understanding of HRM, human learning and behaviour alongside analytical and research methodology skills required to adequately determine the impact of learning and development at work. This area of practice requires a sound grasp of research design because isolating and identifying the effects of training demand careful comparison of trainees with non-trainees, control of confounding variables, and measurement of performance and effectiveness pre- and post-training.

This is another good example of where client organizations understand very effectively what kind of evidence is needed, and require the services of psychologists to provide clarity and expertise about the ways on which evidence should be compiled. In a recent project I led, a local government client in the South East of the UK wanted to evaluate the impact of their high performance leadership development programme. They had made a huge investment in it and made it mandatory for all leaders to attend. Having trained around half of the leaders to date, they wanted to undertake an interim review. The consultancy delivering the training had to date evaluated only the satisfaction and perceptions of the trainees about what they had learned, and whether they had enjoyed the programme. I was engaged to evaluate the impact of the training on actual performance and well-being of staff in the organization (i.e.

were they managed better as a result), as well as the impact on service quality and delivery. It was a hugely complex piece of work, in which a multidisciplinary team of psychologists and statisticians worked with me to collate, analyse and interpret five years of archive data from the organization, and conduct qualitative interviews with various stakeholders. The level of depth of analysis we provided outweighed any superficial examination of training reactions and allowed them to take evidence-based decisions about the next parts of the programme.

Coaching at work

Coaching is a relational form of development that is applied in organizations to address individual development needs. The value of coaching is in the confidential and one-to-one bespoke nature of the development relationship. The issues addressed through coaching are guided by the coachee, and the process of development is facilitative rather than prescriptive. That is, rather than telling coaches what they need to do to improve or address problems at work, the coach rather uses tools and techniques to help the coachee to talk through and work through their performance issues at work and explore solutions and learning activities that will help to solve them.

Coaching shares much of the approach taken by psychologists who work as counsellors and therapists. As a coach, you would need to be non-judgmental, and use questioning, listening and reflecting skilfully to guide solution-focused discussion of the coachee's focal problems. Coaches could be internal or external to an organization, that is, if you wish to practice as a coach, you might do so as an external consultant, or as a member of an organization's development team. Importantly, being a coach is very different from being a mentor. A mentor is usually experienced in a specific career filed or profession, and works with a more junior colleague to provide advice or help career progression. The advice is likely to be directive. Coaching by contrast, does not assume that the coach has more specialist knowledge than the coachee; rather the task is to facilitate self-directed learning through the coaching process, which may comprise goal setting and experiential learning.

The value of coaching has been underlined recently in a meta-analysis, published by the first author of this book, working with colleagues. The research showed for the first time in the scientific literature, the positive impacts of coaching on learning and performance. Specialist training programmes are available for occupational psychologists to develop skills of coaching after their masters training, and the BPS now has a special section on coaching, in moves that point to the increasing professionalization of the field.

Career development

If you are planning on practising in the UK as a psychologist, then we are disappointed to report that it is unlikely that you'll be working directly in career development. It is a painfully under-resourced area of educational and occupational development, despite the fact that at the beginning of working life, the decisions we take about our careers will impact us for the next 60 years, and influence our psychological well-being, productivity and prosperity.

Those psychologists that do work in this area are likely to work one-to-one with clients at various career stages to help them make decisions about their working lives. They typically apply assessment tools, and use their understanding or resources about careers to allow clients to make informed decision and prepare effectively for their chosen careers.

Indirectly, much learning and development activity might be thought of as beneficial for career progression. For example, by working to identify leadership potential among staff on organizations, psychologists are ultimately developing people's careers, promoting specialization along management or technical lines. All training and coaching arguably also contributes to career development through promoting new skills acquisition and inner growth, which in turn promotes progression from one job role to the next.

Skills needed for practice of learning, development and performance management

Reflecting the content of this practice area, the skills you need are varied. For the technical specialisms of performance measurement, training and learning needs analysis, and training evaluation, analytical skills, critical and conceptual skills, and research methodology expertise are needed. As in assessment, the ability to interpret and communicate findings from research is also important. In the practice of training, communication skills are paramount, and organizational and time management competencies are too. Effective training in well organized and planned, and delivered clearly and engagingly. Finally for performance feedback and coaching, listening skills, questioning and one-to-one communication are the most critical. Problem analysis and critical skills are also relevant in order to help address problematic thinking styles or difficult issues on the part of clients.

Organizational development and change

The very substance of organizations is the focus of practice in the area of "OD" (organizational development) and change management. The complexity and multifaceted nature of organizations means that practice in this area is almost always undertaken in multidisciplinary teams. Such teams may include among others specialists in management, marketing and communications, business analysis, finance and economics. Practice in OD can be considered from two perspectives: change management, and proactive OD.

On the management side, practitioner psychologists undertake work to analyse, diagnose and implement organizational change. For example, one mechanism for organizational change is to ensure that recruitment and performance management is such that processes select or reward diversity (i.e. differences in the values, characteristics or competencies) of the people recruited. This could represent a deliberate intervention for change, with psychologists working in multidisciplinary teams to understand the linkages with other organizational functions (e.g. structure and strategy).

Change diagnostics are also key areas of practice for psychologists, undertaken, pre-, during, and post-change. Diagnostics pre-change include identifying areas where change is needed. For example, analytics could be undertaken to determine where significant competency gaps at management level to implement change. Analyses at this level enable psychologists to determine change readiness, the capacity of organizations to undergo and implement change. What is fascinating about diagnostics of change readiness is the impact of contextual factors. The demands on, and nature of each individual business, alongside the purpose or objectives of each organizational change process mean that there is no universal prescription for implementing change in every organization. Psychologists must therefore appreciate and integrate a range of evidence to effectively analyse businesses pre-change.

During change, analyses and interventions are generally designed to weaken resistance and strengthen promoters of change. Social psychological theory and research is highly relevant in this regard. For example, social psychology tells us about how and when attitudes lead to behaviour, and how attitudes might change. Consider an organization wishing to change its safety culture and climate. One of the driving factors of culture and climate is the social norm for behaviour, the informal, often role-model driven actions that represent "the way people do things around here". Through quantitative and qualitative diagnostics, psychologists can identify where resistance and promotion of change reside, and can respectively be addressed or applied.

After a change has been implemented is also an important area for diagnostics. If systems models teach us anything, it is that change in one area of a business inevitably reverberates through other areas. I was engaged as a researcher on a project to examine the impact of a performance management intervention in a UK police service. The change had been implemented approximately 6 months previously, and the objective was to understand the impact. The accounts of officers working under the new systems were informative with respect to, for example, the effects on decision-making, autonomy and discretion. Whilst their compliance with administration increased, many felt a loss of discretion and decision-making latitude in their day to day work. Diagnostics in this vein help to refine and build on interventions to evaluate their effectiveness, and highlight further areas for change.

Beyond diagnostics and change management, practitioners engage in the proactive organizational development. This kind of work applies research and theory at a deeper and more sophisticated level to not only make specific change effective, but also to set up organizations so that they are able to learn about the environments in which they operate in order to adapt quickly and incisively to changes. In this respect, psychologists have a number of strategies that they can implement.

One is organization strategy. Psychologists are concerned with questions around what is strategy, how is it established, and what are the roles of cognition, emotion and social psychology on how it is formed within top management teams? The process of strategy, often wrapped up with the psychology of the management team is an area where the input of psychologists can improve the interactions and mechanisms by which strategy is developed, and refined in an emergent sense.

A second is through staff surveys. Staff surveys are more than just indices of staff satisfaction. When undertaken effectively by psychologists, they provide insight into what areas of an organization or indeed, institution, are working well, and which are not. They help to identify practices that impact on a variety of performance, HR and service-user outcomes. Evidence enables practice to be enhanced in different business areas proactively. An excellent illustration of this is the work undertaken in the UK National Health Service by Michael West and others (see Chapter 3 for an example).

Third, psychologists can work to develop creativity and innovation as core areas of capability. Technological advances occur at such a rate in contemporary business, that they provide limited long-term competitive advantage. As a consequence, the pace of innovation becomes more salient, with creativity and the capacity to implement the products of creative thinking being increasingly valuable, especially where the need for, and nature of change are emergent based on external demands. There is a long history of research in work and organizational psychology on creativity and innovation at work. This research can be applied for example to select more creative people, to identify barriers to innovation, and to develop work systems that promote and reward innovation.

Fourth, work and organizational psychologists can proactively develop team-working in organizations. There is a strong intersection of research on team-working and diversity management. This is because teams are the receptacles within which interactions, co-working, and performance of different people play out. People may be diverse on many demographic and psychological characteristics, and team design and team management processes have an impact on the social, well-being, and performance outcomes of the team. In respect of change, team diversity is important to consider. Research shows that diversity leads to positive effectiveness outcomes when tasks are complex and require multiple perspectives to problem solve. Lack of diversity could by contrast hinder adaptation to change, with team member strengths and characteristics suited rather to a fixed or limited set of performance demands. Where the nature of change is uncertain (as is the case with emergent change), preparing teams for change through diversity management represents an important proactive strategy.

A fifth strategy is to embed organizational learning systems. This is a highly sophisticated approach to managing organizational knowledge and decision-making. Learning organizations have a good grasp of their environment and health, much like learning, living organisms. In the case of organizations, this insight is likely to be data-driven, based on metrics of all kinds within the organization. This is an area of Occupational Psychology practice that intersects with the trend of so-called "Big Data" in the digital economy. In the future, we can expect the steps already taken in behavioural analytics of Big Data to be more and more influential in the work of psychologists.

Learning organizations are also perceived as holding grounds for knowledge. Psychologists have an important part to play in management and organization of knowledge in a business. For example, how does an organization ensure that tacit knowledge (implicit expertise) is retained in an organization after the person that holds the knowledge leaves? Knowledge and expertise are arguably the most critical assets an organization holds in navigating change and development. By designing organizational systems, processes and structures in such a way that knowledge is shared, and thereby retained and applied more effectively, psychologists are able to ready businesses for continual change.

Skills needed for practice of organizational development and change

OD and change are messy areas of work and organizational psychology, and they require therefore a tolerance of ambiguity, and a level of flexibility and adaptability that is arguably higher than in other areas of practice. Practitioners who prefer more certainty and data-driven conclusiveness in respect of practice are better advised to select an alternative specialism. Alongside this general style, complex problem solving and an ability to communicate clearly and effectively at the very highest level of organizational management are advantageous.

Workplace health & well-being

This topic, as in many other areas in which occupational psychologists are involved, encompasses a range of activities i.e. dealing with stress and at one end of the spectrum to positive psychology at the other.

An interesting definition of stress is produced by the UK's Health and Safety Executive: "the process that arises where work demands of various types and combinations exceed the person's capacity and capability to cope".

This is interesting in a number of ways:

First, there is an individual difference component to it as it depends upon each person's "capacity and capability". What is stressful for one person therefore may not be to another.

Second, all of us can experience stress. The concept itself borrows from other disciplines such as physics and engineering, and relates to a load that is placed upon an object. Each of us has, or will, experience stress and strain – it just requires the right combination of factors.

Third, though is the source of the definition itself, the Health and Safety Executive (HSE). This reveals a number of points. The topic of stress, as in many areas of occupational psychology, can be considered from a number of different perspectives. In many organizations, stress is a Health and Safety issue. This clearly has consequences in terms of the way it is perceived. Stress is something that is unhealthy and negative but because of this is also something that organizations do not like drawing attention to.

Nevertheless, psychologists have an important contribution to make to this area, both in terms of diagnosis and recommendations for its reduction.

There is now a well-developed body of knowledge within psychology about the demands which can lead to stress. The HSE has drawn upon this and has identified six work-related factors:

Demands – the expected performance requirements;
Control – the power to affect their performance;

Support – of others, training given, resources;
Role – clarity versus ambiguity;
Relationships – with key people, especially teams;
Change – how much change is occurring – members and line managers.

Generally speaking, we need some pressure at work to achieve optimal performance. Too much pressure leads to burn out, too little to rust out.

Finding the "sweet spot" is where psychologists can play an important role. In researching stress at work you would typically use a mix of qualitative and quantitative methods. Surveys and questionnaires are readily available. The HSE survey tool is available free of charge but consultants and OPs who specialize in this field have also developed their own. Typically, a survey-led approach will provide an overview of the relative presence of each of the key factors in the workplace. This is obviously good to know. Such data will also enable a comparison to be made of different parts of the organization so particular "hot spots" can be identified.

To delve deeper into the specifics of each of the demands requires richer data and this will most often be obtained by qualitative methods such as interviews and/or focus groups. This data will enable more specific issues to be located and highlighted. This following example gives an idea of the type of activity psychologists get involved in.

The organization, a large public sector body, had many regional and local offices. With each region there was a small group of people who were responsible for bringing about a specific change within the organization. Over the course of the year 80% of the people had left their roles. Some had left the organization completely, others had transferred to different roles within the same organization. As a first step a stress and well-being survey was conducted with a number of people who had been in roles for at least six months. The survey demonstrated that individuals were experiencing very high loads of pressure across a number of areas, most notably as role clarity and support.

Interviews were conducted with approximately 20 people across the organization. These revealed a number of factors:

- Too few resources for the teams to carry out their work and achieve their objectives.

- Lack of understanding from the management about the nature of their work. This is what led to the setting of objectives which were not achievable.
- Reporting structures were inappropriate. The teams were not integrated into the management structures and were seen as something different to, and a distraction from, day-to-day business.

In addition, the interviews also revealed the impact this was having on the individuals themselves. The people in these roles had been chosen because of their record of success in their previous positions. They were seen, and saw themselves, as achievers, people who got things done. To be in a position where they were not successful had a corresponding impact on their own self-confidence. Their record of previous success also meant that they had accepted the objectives that had been set for the role when they accepted it – they had the self-believe to think they would succeed and this came from their previous experience.

So, whilst the survey undoubtedly helped ascertain what the overall picture was, the interviews helped to provide the detail

The recommendations were a mix of changing the job role, establishing achievable but stretching targets and providing additional support, especially in terms of training. There was a willingness, on the part of the organization to see this as a broader structural issue rather than treating it as a problem with the individuals and their inability to deal with the pressures. Clearly, the issue had reached a crisis point with its high level of staff turnover and so a rethink was required.

So you can see the in-depth qualitative approaches illustrated the specific issues that needed to be addressed. In our experience, stress-related subjects are those that organizations would prefer to steer clear of; firstly because of its negative connotations, but secondly because of potential litigation and reputational damage.

Focussing on stress can also mean that we fail to look at other emotional features of the workplace that increase job satisfaction and engagement. Again, psychologists have an important contribution to make to discussions on these topics and have been taken seriously by organizations because they have demonstrated links with productivity, although some research disputes this. Nevertheless, job satisfaction is seen by organizations to be a good thing. Not surprisingly, the absence of the factors that cause stress can help lead to job satisfaction. Being empowered, having control of your work, having stretching but achievable objectives and working in a supportive environment all increase job satisfaction. Leadership style undoubtedly has an impact.

Nor should we underestimate the significance of being fairly treated to satisfaction and engagement. Pay and remuneration is an indication of value but it is not the most important one for many people. It is more about recognition of their worth and acknowledgement of their contribution to a team's success. Fairness, furthermore, is not just something that is related to diversity. Being unfairly treated is something that evokes strong emotions in many people. Psychologists have a key role not in just increasing job satisfaction but in creating the conditions (e.g., fairness in measuring performance, and in promotion systems) that contribute to higher job satisfaction.

The work on engagement and satisfaction is now part of HR, so any occupational psychologists should expect to work as part of a multidisciplinary team. Occupational psychologists do have a distinct perspective to bring to the topic. The evidence-based approach, drawing upon many key theories in psychology, e.g., motivation, equality, assessment, bring depth to a topic that can often be treated somewhat superficially.

Influencing policy & strategy

The extent to which psychologists influence policy and strategy depends on how they see their role. Too often, occupational psychologists can see themselves as technical experts, in particular, on the topics of selection and assessment. Clearly, within these areas, the views of the psychologists will be central to formulating policy.

The areas that occupational psychologists work in overlap considerably with HR specialists, learning and development specialists as well as others who will have responsibility for specific aspects of people management.

So, to influence the broader aspects of people strategy (and let's stick with this for the moment) means being able to influence colleagues with a different set of experiences and priorities. In such situations, each person needs to decide: Am I a psychologist or one of the crowd?

Being able to stand apart and have your skills and experience recognized is a critical step in being able to influence others. This clearly is addressed to those how work as internal consultants rather than those they bring in as external experts.

The next step is to determine what approach is the best to persuade those around us.

Robbins et al. (2012) reviewed the literature on influence and persuasion and identified a number of strategies:

Legitimacy: relying on authority or stressing that a request is in accordance with organizational policies or roles.

Inspirational appeals: developing emotional commitment by appealing to people's values, needs, hopes and aspirations.

Consultation: Inviting the person or people in the decision and/or how a change should be implemented and accomplished.

Exchange: rewarding the person with favours and benefits in exchange for following a request.

Personal appeals: asking for compliance based on friendship or loyalty.

Ingratiation: using flattery, praise or friendly behaviour prior to making a request.

Pressure: using warning, repeated demands and threats.

Coalition: using the support of other people to persuade the target.

The effectiveness of the technique depends on the direction of influence.

Upward Influence	Downward Influence	Lateral Influence
● Rational Persuasion	● Rational persuasion	● Rational persuasion
	● Inspirational appeals	● Consultation
	● Pressure	● Ingratiation
	● Consultation	● Exchange
	● Ingratiation	● Legitimacy
	● Exchange	● Personal appeals
	● Legitimacy	● Coalition

The one approach that worked well across all levels of influence was rational persuasion. For downward influence and lateral influence a number of other techniques worked.

It is likely that a combination of approaches will be most effective, nevertheless, to influence policy and strategy will invariably mean upward and lateral influencing. In these cases, rational persuasion worked with both categories. This brings us back to the earlier discussion in Chapter 3 of values and EBM, Evidence Based Management. To influence policy and strategy means, being confident about our knowledge base. As an occupational psychologist, it is important that you are able to distinguish between what Briner and Rousseau call "Best Practice" and "Best Evidence". This, in turn, means being open-minded and agnostic about what the "best" way forward is. Inevitably, we all have our own views about what we would like to do; we will be influenced by the desired approvals of our colleagues and managers. Nevertheless, this may not constitute best evidence. Best practice in often in organizations is based on "what other organizations are doing". For example, colleagues will review most of what the organization's key competitors are doing on given topics. It is discovered that Banks A, B and C were all doing much the same thing. These actions will then be considered to be "best practice". However, Bank B may have taken an action because Bank A was doing it and Bank C only did it because Banks A and B were doing it. Best practice may not represent anything more than common practice – which is not the same thing at all.

So, to influence policy and strategy, OPs need to use rational persuasion which requires an understanding of the theoretical and research-based actions which we can draw up on. Failure to do this will limit an OPs effectiveness in influencing policy and strategy beyond a technical offering.

Influencing policy and strategy also requires occupational psychologists to have a broader understanding of an organization's wider mission, vision and goals. The work of the Civil Service psychologists provide an interesting case in point: psychologists are used not only to inform policy and strategy, but also to achieve the overall goals that the Civil Service wishes to achieve. Influencing policy and strategy requires alignment of

- Personal goals and values
- Professional expertise and evidence
- Organization vision, mission and goals

When this occurs and by application of a rational persistent approach the impact an OP has will be considerably enhanced.

Diversity management

Many large organizations, particularly in North America and the UK, have diversity policies. These have their origins in the equal opportunities policies which the most progressive organizations began developing in the 1970. This was in response to Civil Rights and anti-discrimination legislation in the US and Europe.

In the 1980's, the emphasis shifted from legal compliance to examining the composition of the workforce in response to the changing demographics in the population. In this regard a key report was Workforce 2000 which showed how the population in America was going to change by the start of the new millennium. Whilst many were interested in the subject at a personal level, psychologists had been slow to recognize this as an area they could contribute to.

So what is managing diversity? The basic concept of managing diversity accepts that the workforce consists of a diverse population of people. The diversity consist of visible and non-visible differences which will include sex, age, background, race, disability, personality and workstyle. It is founded on the premise that harnessing these differences will create a productive environment in which everybody feels valued, where their talents are being fully utilized and in which organizations goals are met.

There are many ways in which OP can contribute to diversity management in meaningful ways which add value to practice and strategy. At a process level OPs can examine the extent to which the processes which are operated in organizations are fair and objective. A notable area is that of selection and much time and energy has been spent on looking at the fairness of different aspects of selection. The extent to which the results of academic research are translated into OP practice can be disappointing: the emphasis for many practitioners is on following the practices which ensure reliability and validity with not so much concern for fairness of approaches. This is not to say that psychology can provide the answers. The adverse impact of selection tests for example remains a particularly knotty problem with no easy resolutions.

Another key area where OPs have made a difference in diversity management is the subject of unconscious bias. Over the decades, and more markedly over the last 50 years, the proportion of people who endorse prejudice, e.g. racist or sexist comments, has fallen markedly. This, we believe, is despite the protestations of some writers, a good thing. The reduction of sexist and racist remarks and behaviour undoubtedly makes daily life easier for most people.

Despite this however, the diversity at senior levels in organizations has changed very little. Psychologists have successfully identified the challenge in organizations is to tackle unconscious bias – the biases we didn't know we had. The work on bias can take many forms e.g. OPs carry out reviews of talent identification and promotion processes. Whilst the data-gathering approaches may not be too different from those mentioned elsewhere in this book (i.e. surveys, interviews, focus groups). The type of data they collect (i.e. the questions being asked) and more significantly the framework for analysis are critical. In order to conduct such work effectively an OP needs to understand the key theories and research to provide a deeper level of analysis to the client. For example, in one project looking at gender in an organization there were a number of issues, some of which are described below. The primary means of gathering views of employees was focus groups.

First, some people, all women, felt that men and women had different skills and that the organization was fair to appreciate the female skillset. Second, other women said that they felt stereotyped and were not judged on their performance objectively. Third, men in the organization felt that flexible working policies were designed for women and they were less likely to be granted flexible working requests.

It would be easy to see these as separate issues. However, they are all linked by the issue of stereotypes. The first two points relate to descriptive stereotypes and the third point to prescriptive stereotypes. The women who believe that men and women have different strengths are merely perpetuating age-old stereotypes in a positive way.

The second point, in some ways is a re-articulation, but is a more negative version of the first point. The issue the men raised, however, the third point, related to the prescription of the roles men and women should adopt i.e. the male should be the breadwinner and the female the homemaker. The policy was a gender neutral policy i.e. it is for all staff. The way it was adopted however, demonstrated underlying stereotypical attitudes. Therefore to address this merely as a problem in the way a policy is applied misses the deeper and more fundamental issue – the way we view men and women's roles at work and at home. It is the insights that psychology provides that enables OPs to bring a fresh perspective to issues that many organizations have found difficult to resolve despite their best efforts.

Training of staff is another way that OPs can assist in diversity management. The issue of unconscious bias is a good example of the direct application of psychology to workplace settings.

The other ways in which psychologists can make a difference is to challenge existing practice using best evidence. There is within the field of diversity management an orthodox set of actions which have come to be considered as good practice. The evidence for some of these actions can be somewhat sketchy to say the least.

It is accepted by many organizations, for example, that they need to construct a "business case" for diversity. Reports have been compiled showing, for example, the business case for having more women on non-executive boards. One report produced by the Department for Business Information and Skills showed how the research was conclusive: women on boards produce better results for organizations. The problem with this analysis, however, is that it is incorrect. The research that was presented ignored results that showed diversity made no difference and other research that showed diversity was detrimental to performance. We have stressed the importance of evidence-based policy, well this is an example of what is referred, in some circles, as policy-based evidence. In other words, using the evidence that supports the story you want to tell and ignoring rest.

By not being open to all the research present and from not asking more pertinent questions: in this case why is diversity a good thing in some instances and a bad thing in others? The answer to this question likes in whether people feel valued and included. Whilst the research on diversity is mixed, the research on inclusion demonstrates for more positive outcomes.

The work on inclusion has led to increasing attention being paid to the role of leaders in diversity management. Inclusive leadership therefore is another way OPs can work with organizations, to help managers and leaders of people to get the best out of their teams by adopting a genuinely inclusive approach.

The approaches that are adapted in organizations today with regards to diversity management are much the same as those adopted twenty or more years ago. The orthodoxy, or "Best Practice" approach has led to an ossification of the field. There can be few areas of management which have changed so little for over two decades and which still seem resistant to challenge.

Psychology and OPs have an opportunity to bring different approaches, perspectives and solutions to bear because whilst practice has not altered the world is changing. Concepts such as intersectionality and super-diversity will challenge diversity practitioners as much as criticisms of the slow rate of progress on diversity management.

Leadership & management

These are two areas where OPs have had an impact, and in many respects have great opportunities to do more.

Leadership, at its core, is about enabling a groups of people to achieve a set of objectives. The leader needs to influence the group or team to do what is required to achieve the goals or vision.

Management is typically seen as the resource that is required to implement the plans and strategies to achieve the goal.

Leadership is seen as being more strategic, having a clearer view on the longer-term vision and objectives. Management is seen as more operational – less concerned with the bigger picture but more focussed on the here and now.

Of course, in practice many of these lines become blurred. Some people are in positions of leadership because it is expected of the role (i.e. an issue of status). Of course, managers will also be leaders of their own teams and they will have to galvanize, moderate, direct and inspire their team to achieve goals.

There are many skills that leaders and manager have. One model, which also illustrates how OPs have approached leadership and management, has clustered leadership into three different but overlapping areas. Thought Leadership, Task Leadership and People Leadership (Pearn Kandola, 2015; see Figure 4.1.)

* **People Leadership:** The people leader inspires others towards achievement of ambitious goals through a combination of communication, influencing and engagement skills. They are openly

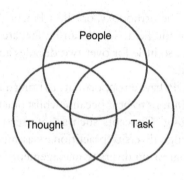

Figure 4.1 Pearn Kandola iLead Model

passionate about what they aim to achieve, yet caring and consider-
ate in the way that they approach others. They know that people
are their most valuable resource and will do their utmost to secure
and retain the commitment of their teams.

- **Task Leadership:** The task leader drives others towards achievement of ambitious goals through a combination of determination,
  resilience and clarity of focus. They take ultimate responsibility for
  the quality and delivery of results, and are highly skilled in the way
  that they delegate tasks and ensure that others are aware of the priority targets. They optimize performance and realize the full talents
  of the people around them in achieving results.
- **Thought Leadership:** The thought leader constantly looks to new
  opportunities and the future. They quickly evaluate complex and
  ambiguous situations and are ready to analyse and challenge tough
  decisions. The thought leader initiates changes and improvements,
  and is imaginative and open to taking entrepreneurial risk.

There are many other related definitions, but generally speaking this
framework covers the broad areas that leaders and managers need to
consider. At one level OPs work with organizations to help them identify leaders. This means having effective, valid and fair processes to
identify people who have potential to be leaders of the future. This in
fact is one of the most important things that an organization must do
to ensure stability and continued success: create a plan of succession so
that should something happen to one of the key players in a business,

there will always be somebody ready to step into the role. OPs do this by helping with, for example, development centres. The format is based around that of assessment centres and it will share many features with it, most notably multiple assessors, multiple participants and multiple methods. The key difference lies in the feel and the orientation of the development centre. More feedback is given to the participants and more coaching will be involved. The output may well be a "yes" or "no" decision about whether somebody is suitable for a more senior role, but more typically a decision will be made about a person's readiness for a leadership role. Some may be ready immediately, other may be ready in two or more years. In each case, however, participants will be told how they performed, their strengths and development areas and an indication of the skills they need to work on to be more effective now and in the future.

The emphasis has shifted over the last two decades from individuals being assessed by a group of remote figures of involving psychologists, to a situation where the participant and psychologist work together in a more collaborative fashion to identify ways to improve the person's overall effectiveness.

Coaching is obviously involved in such work, but even without development centres, OPs are involved in working one-to-one with leaders and also working with a leadership team. Despite the competition that exists from other people, psychologists appear to be highly regarded as coaches due to the extra insight they can bring to the relationship. The best psychologists involved in coaching will use a blend of formal training, psychological theory and experience to help clients in a wide variety of ways. The best OP coaches have the flexibility to adapt to virtually every situation that they are faced with and if they have not they use the experience to learn from for the future.

Psychologists will also be involved in designing succession and talent management programmes, so that people are being evaluated in an objective, valued and fair way.

In addition to this, however, psychology offers a lot to the actual *skills* that are requested of leaders and managers. For example, the iLead Toolkit for Leaders identified many ways in which psychology can be used to develop a wide range of leadership capabilities listing the following skills.

People	Task	Thought
How to motivate others	How to take responsibility	How to develop strategic long-term goals
How to raise energy levels	How to deliver every time	How to be innovative
How to be assertive	How to take control	How to think about problems laterally
How to influence others	How to know when and how to take risks	How to reframe problems
How to develop rapport	How to maintain momentum	How to prioritize tasks ready for action
How to communicate effectively	How to cope with setbacks	How to make timely decisions
How to actively listen	How to formulate action plans	How to focus on the bigger picture
How to manage your impact	How to win and manage resources	How to make complex ideas simple, clear and concise
How to manage difficult conversations	How to communicate your vision	How to make ethical decisions
How to create team identity	How to delegate	How to make reasoned judgements
How to build and maintain trust	How to engage others to deliver	How to direct people
How to gain buy-in and commitment	How to build resilience	How to improve processes
How to support and challenge in tandem	How to use optimism to achieve	How to be confident in making judgement calls
How to give feedback	How to get the most out of yourself	How to challenge other effectively
How to identify your personal meaning		How to balance risk with potential benefits
How to be an effective role model		
How to identify personal learning styles		
How to develop others		

Research

With Occupational Psychology being a scientific discipline and the applied approach taken by psychologists being centred on a scientist-practitioner model, research features to some extent in all practice domains. That research might be desk-based research in order to investigate a focal client problem, or primary research gathering and analysing data as part of practitioner work. We have highlighted some specific areas where this might apply.

However, in this section, we focus exclusively on academic applied research as a realm of practice of psychologists. There has always been a strong academic community in work and organizational psychology as a discipline. Attending research-led conferences such as the IWP conference in the UK, the EAWOP conference in Europe, and the SIOP conference in the US is testament to this fact. Academic researchers are almost exclusively employed in universities, and may be employed specifically as research staff, or full academic faculty.

Research staff tend to have a title like Research Fellow, or Research Associate/Assistant. Their role is to undertake research under the direction and supervision of a more senior academic. Psychologists in these roles typically work on a defined project led by the senior academic, who will make decisions about the objectives and purpose of the research, and how and in what ways it will be undertaken. Projects of this kind tend to be funded by a sponsor, which might be a research foundation or council (who fund academic research on behalf of the government or charities, for example), or organizations (public or private sector organizations for example, who have need for research to be undertaken on an applied issue or need). On this track of research practice, psychologists work to carry out research, collaborating with research participants and sponsors, to deliver on project objectives. In addition to technical research tasks, dissemination and communication of findings to different audiences, and in different forms (e.g. in reports, presentations, online and media) all feature in the role.

Where do Occupational Psychologists work?

There are technically no limits to where an OP can work, and indeed as a graduate of an Occupational Psychology programme, you can enter the working world through the usual graduate routes. You may there-fore find people with OP backgrounds in various different organiza-tions and roles.

Practitioner Occupational Psychologists however, tend to be clus-tered into three kinds of work situations: internal in organizations, in consultancies or in Universities.

Internal Posts in Organizations. Generally, teams of OPs are likely to work in larger organizations because the scope of their contribution is wider. Small and medium size businesses are less likely to employ a psychologist, and would instead access services of consultants.

Working in an organization has the benefit of greater job security typically, and you are able to work with other OP colleagues, supported by the resources of a large organizational employer. If being in a large or prestigious corporate is of value to you, then this kind of work envi-ronment is where to aim. There are examples in the public and private sectors. For example in the public sector, as we earlier highlighted, the Civil Service employs many psychologists across different Departments. The Department for Work and Pensions for example has a team of OPs, who have opportunity to work on initiatives for personnel and HRM internally, as well as contribute to policy. The Ministry of Defence also employ OPs as part of their management structures.

In the private sector, notable examples of companies where there are teams of psychologists include Shell, EDF and RBS in the UK. There are also examples of larger organizational settings where OP teams form part of the company through acquisition. An example was the acquisition of SHL (a test publisher employing mainly psychologists) by CEB in 2012. Finally, whilst corporates may not always hire whole teams of OPs, it is common for multi-nationals to hire individual OPs to be part of specialist teams (e.g. working on recruitment and perfor-mance management for example).

Consultancy. Most practising OPs work in consultancies. These may be specialist OP firms or more general consultancies. Here we focus on the OP specialist specifically. The size of consultancies varies signifi-cantly, and will influence of course your experience of working in them. They may be micro businesses of a few people, in which case you will find opportunity to really make a difference to the company and work on a wide variety of things. Or they may be more established employ-ing 20–50 consultants, and have a bigger client base and operations that are more formalized. There are also multi-national consultancies of OPs working globally (a good example is Cubiks, operating across the world, and employing hundreds of work and organizational psychologists). Other example consultancies include Pearn Kandola, and Work Psychology Group.

Universities. With their scientific background and natural interest and inclination towards research, it is little wonder that many OPs work in Universities. There are two main tracks of career for OPs in Universities. One is to work as a research-active academic, conducting and publishing research. Research projects may be applied projects that have impact in terms of changing policy or organizations. A core activity of research-active psychologists though is to contribute to knowledge through publishing research papers. Academic jobs also involve teaching students, including those on OP MSc programmes. The second track is focused exclusively on teaching students, without a requirement to undertake or publish research.

Global working

Occupational Psychology is a profession with truly global reach. It is the norm for OPs to be travelling and working internationally, especially when they work in consultancy. International working may involve various kinds of work assignment. Short-term assignments involve working on projects for days or weeks with international clients. Longer-term assignments are more traditionally *expatriate* assignments where an OP may be tasked with setting up or leading an international operation of a consultancy.

A third kind of international working is enabled through advances in digital services. Virtual international working involves providing digital service such as online testing internationally, or for example, licensing products (training programmes, assessment centres, well-being tools etc) to international partners. Relationships between OPs in different countries can be managed virtually through video-conferencing, and increasingly through SMS or messaging services. These tools bring together international project teams very straightforwardly.

Your experience of the international nature of work and organizational psychology will begin during you MSc year. Your course colleagues will be from many different countries, it is not unusual on a

20-student programme to have a dozen or more countries represented. This is a wonderful opportunity to learn and make connections across the globe, and we encourage you to do all you can to work in diverse groups on activities such as presentations or class assignments.

Working with international class mates is also important because it begins your development of intercultural competencies. These are competencies that enable effective communication and interpersonal interactions with people from different and diverse cultural backgrounds (such as listening, dropping our assumptions about others, asking questions, withholding judgement), and there have been increasing calls for these to be included in the OP curriculum (see e.g. Griffith & Wang, 2010). To work globally effectively requires an understanding of working across cultures, and once you have developed this, personally speaking, you will find it a joy, and privilege of the profession.

Entrepreneurship in Occupational Psychology

There is one key difference between Occupational Psychology and clinical and educational psychology areas and that is that there is no obvious single or dominant employment route for OPs.

Clinical psychologists will work in the NHS principally and an educational psychologist's work will be with education authorities. There is no clearly defined route for OP and so there are a number of career options. Many OPs however, will be self-employed and so the topic of entrepreneurship is one of particular interest.

Being self-employed and being entrepreneurial are not necessarily the same. For example, some people become self-employed because they many have been made redundant from a previous role. For many OPs, it is a conscious decision to start their own business. This section looks at what we mean by entrepreneurship and what this means for OPs.

Starting a business

Here, we do not go into the details, legal and financial, of how to set up a business. It is important to think about the decision carefully and take appropriate advice, for example from solicitors and accountants. You will need to create a mission and business plan and to forecast revenues and costs.

It is something of a myth that only people who have their own business can be called an entrepreneur. There seems to be such a strong desire in society to have only one idea of an entrepreneur that it can appear almost ideological. Research shows that some managers within organizations display the same qualities of the most effective business owners. So this chapter will have applicability to OPs who find themselves working in organizations. But given the high proportion of OPs who will be self-employed our focus here is on what this means in practice.

An entrepreneur is defined as someone "who creates and manages a business in an innovative way" (McKenna, 2012, p261).

Saville Consulting's Wave Personality Profile system has a number of dimensions related to what they refer to as Entrepreneurial Potential. Their model is based on the research of David Hall and his team at Entrecode. Overall there are 6 core areas, each of which is broken down further, providing 21 aspects of entrepreneurial potential. Table 4.1 provides an overview of the model.

One of the key aspects of this model is an underlying belief that entrepreneurs are not born, they are made. By doing the right things people have the capability to be entrepreneurial.

Getting in the zone focusses on the willingness to act as well as understanding what they want to achieve as an individual and as a business.

Seeing possibilities involves keeping an eye on the big picture and not getting too bogged down, or for too long on the detail. It can be very easy for example for OPs to work on filling their diaries for the new to short-term. The desire to do this is understandable, after all there are bills to pay and who knows when the work will dry up. In fact becoming too busy in the short-term will, in many instances, lead to a drop in activity later as relativity little time will be available for developing the business in the future. But being "savvy" is also important, i.e. using experience and intuition to help create opportunities rather than relying on data. This may be seen to be at odds with an evidence-based approach and certainly some of the academics who advocate EBM, may find this unpalatable.

Table 4.1 Key characteristics of entrepreneurs.

Core Areas	Aspects
Getting in the Zone	● Achievement drive ● Compelling vision ● Energy ● Action orientated
Seeing Possibilities	● Big picture ● Options Thinking ● Savvy
Creating Superior Opportunities	● Problem seeking ● Synthesis ● Problem solving ● Delighting customers
Staying in the Zone	● Focus ● Positive Mindset ● Self – determining ● Persistence
Opening up to the World	● Expressing passion ● Purposeful networking ● Creating partnership
Building Capability	● Building up the team ● Experiential learning ● Staying on track

They are not necessarily incompatible however. Listening to client concerns for example can often be the clue that is needed to explore a hunch or idea by reviewing the psychological research and theory.

Creating superior opportunities involves listening to clients and finding solutions that help to solve their problems. For an OP the solutions *have* to be psychologically orientated, otherwise why would anyone invite an OP in. For example, take this client problem. A university café is facing increasing competition from larger chains opening nearby, as well as more boutique and specialist coffee shops. In addition, there is a problem with queuing at peak times, leading to complaints particularly from students. So, that's the problem, how would you go about solving it? In fact, this is a problem that we regularly pose to students studying Occupational Psychology. Their first response is to come up with ideas to reduce the queues, e.g. hire more staff, and change the queuing system. It often involves conducting a survey of the customers: what do they want from the cafeteria? And so on. The question then put to the students is "Did the client really need a psychologist to tell them that? Of course not". So here we have a group of intelligent, highly committed people that have spent time and increasing amounts of money to become an OP, yet at the first problem that they are faced with they put all of that knowledge, expense and training to one side to become a non-specific lay person. It's a strikingly anomalous position. The barriers to entry to become a consultant are low. To become a chartered OP however, requires an undergraduate degree, a postgraduate degree plus at least two years' experience. This requires motivation, dedication and persistence. It also provides you with specialist skills and knowledge. With this particular problem we asked the students to rethink the problem this time using relevant psychological theory and research. This guides them to what data will be gathered as well as providing a framework for considering the solution. Just to remind you: there's nothing as practical as a good theory.

Staying in the zone is about persistence, focus and remaining positive. Owning your own business comes with many advantages, specifically in terms of control and empowerment. However, as in any field there are problems that arise. There is the longer-term economic cycle which happens every decade or so where there will be a recession, some deeper than others. In between these longer-term cycles businesses can experience their own difficulties. Staying focussed and having a belief in your abilities is important.

Opening up to the world refers to expressing passion, networking and creating partnerships. It is important whatever you choose to specialize in that you are able to communicate your skills and expertise to clients and potential clients. There is no point having the world's greatest mousetrap if no-one knows about it. Networking is one of those words that can make OPs feel uncomfortable. It is not just about meeting people and being prepared to talk about yourself and your services. It is important to find ways of networking or communicating with others that you feel comfortable with. This could include giving talks, attending conferences, writing articles, etc. Whatever, you do you will need to be sharp, distinctive and clear in communicating what you offer.

A lot of work in the public sector is now open to public tender. Learning about these opportunities is important, so scanning relevant databases is a necessary activity. But having done that you need to write proposals that convey your capabilities succinctly and accurately. One common mistake however when writing a proposal is to provide a list of features e.g.

- I am an occupational psychologist
- I have conducted research into the specific topics you wish to address.
- The method suggested here is systematic and reliable.

The client is not necessarily interested in this. Instead what they want to know is what this means for them. So, using a short linking phrase "which means that . . . . . ." helps to turn a feature into a benefit.

"I am an Occupational Psychologist" becomes "I am an Occupational Psychologist which means that I am well qualified and highly trained with the experience you need".

Try using that phase with the other two features.

Building Capacity involves creating, developing and motivating a team; experiential learning and staying on track. The team element ensures that the team has the skills and capabilities needed to deliver the desired outcomes to a client. In addition, OPs will need to learn from their experiences and be prepared to try out new things. Staying on track involves continuous improvement and one way to do this is to get feedback from colleagues and clients at the end of a project about how well it was carried out. Project reviews, as well as client feedback all feed into making processes of project management and delivery more efficient.

Being entrepreneurial is not inconsistent or antithetical to being professional. It means always acknowledging and respecting the theoretical and research base of psychology. It also means keeping up to date with the latest developments and thinking. As an OP you will specialize in two or three areas within the field. The evidence-based management approach means that you should be doing regular reviews in your areas of expertise every few years. One result of these reviews is that it will increase your knowledge and may lead to improvements in the way you provide solutions to clients. It is a complaint that is regularly heard from practitioners that they do not have the time to carry out the work required to keep up to date. As an excuse it is not good enough. It will take time and effort but it also means enhancing what you have to offer and make your business more resilient in the face of the demands that you face in a competitive marketplace. In other words: Don't be lazy!

5 | How to become an Occupational Psychologist

If you are reading this far in the book, then we assume that you have decided a) that Occupational Psychology is very probably the right specialist career in psychology for you, and b) that the subjects you learn about, and the practice work you do as an Occupational Psychologist is interesting and appealing to you.

The next key question you to answer is "how?" How do you become an Occupational Psychologist?

Before explaining what you need to do, we want you to recall something we highlighted earlier. Becoming an Occupational Psychologist requires that you want to *master* the discipline and join the profession as a registered specialist practitioner psychologist. In practice, this means that the training is stretching, and requires commitment, perseverance, proactivity and dedication. So be prepared to work hard.

The training to be an Occupational Psychologist is best thought of as a pathway. For all specialisms of psychology in the UK, a first step is to attain Graduate Basis for Chartered Membership with the BPS, usually through a first degree (Bachelors) in psychology (see www.bps.org.uk), but also through an accredited conversion qualification. Afterwards, the training proceeds as follows:

1   Complete a BPS-accredited Master's Degree in Occupational or Work and Organizational Psychology (Stage 1).
2   Complete the BPS Stage 2 Qualification in Occupational Psychology (comprising at least 2 years of supervised practice), or alternative equivalent qualification recognized by the Health and Care Professions Council.

3   Apply to the Health and Care Professions Council to register as an Occupational Psychologist.

This Chapter guides you through the steps of the training pathway.

Stage 1: the Master's degree

Choosing a programme

Qualifying Masters degrees are accredited by the BPS. There are many institutions offering accredited Masters programmes across the UK, and you should obviously choose one that is right for you in terms of cost and location. However, when choosing a programme, it is also worth keeping a number of points in mind.

Degree Title: Not all accredited Masters will be titled Occupational Psychology. Work and/or Organizational Psychology are also popular titles and provided they are accredited by the BPS, will enable you to become and Occupational Psychologist.

Psychology Department or Business School: It is very common for Masters degrees in Occupational Psychology to be hosted in business schools rather than psychology departments in Universities. Work and organizational psychology has arguably much stronger overlaps with organizational behaviour and human resource management than with for example, cognitive neuroscience. This means that work and organizational psychologists normally find a better fit for their work in schools of business rather than in psychology groups. Given that our clients are from organizations and businesses, an academic environment in which they train as managers is also conducive to understanding their needs and perspectives. Box 5.1 lists a number of prominent business schools in the UK offering accredited programmes in Occupational Psychology at the time of writing.

Box 5.1

Aston Business School: MSc Work Psychology and Business
Leeds University Business School: MSc Organizational Psychology
Manchester Business School: MSc Organizational Psychology

> Sheffield Management School: MSc Occupational Psychology
> Surrey Business School: MSc Occupational and Organizational
>   Psychology

School Reputation: It is a good idea to consult University rankings (e.g. Guardian, Times, National Student Survey, Research Excellence Rankings) to get a feel for the experience that you will have, and the standing of the institution.

Academic Faculty (i.e. programme staff): This is potentially the most important factor to consider, yet is the one that few students really look into. *Who* is going to lead your classes and facilitate your learning? What are their specialisms, and are they consistent with your interests?

Academic departments will not have world experts in every aspect of Occupational Psychology. Rather they will tend to cluster around key themes or areas of expertise that are emphasized in each particular school. You should seek to understand the strengths of each school on your shortlist, and check that you will be taught by professors and teachers who are leading in their field, credible, qualified and experienced.

Positive indicators about programme faculty include:

- Large group of research-active staff (check their recent publications) specializing in work and organizational psychology, or relevant areas of organizational behaviour and HRM.
- Dedicated teaching staff with applied (corporate/industry) experience supporting the programme – this helps immensely in enriching your understanding of how Occupational Psychology is applied.
- Themes of research in the school that match your own particular interests.
- Professors or staff with whom you are interested to work closely, for example, on your dissertation.

Potentially negative signs about programme faculty:

- Few or zero research-active staff (this means that while you may still hear about up-to-date research, you will not receive perspectives from those *shaping* the field).

- Small group of work and organizational psychologists, surrounded by staff from unrelated disciplines (e.g. medical disciplines, experimental or neuropsychology).
- Module teaching led by inexperienced faculty (this may indicate that the school is not investing heavily in work and organizational psychology).
- Staff seem to have little practical experience of applying Occupational Psychology.

The Master's degree structure

We covered the curriculum (what you learn about) in depth in Chapter 2. The seven knowledge areas will form the basis of all accredited Masters programmes. However, keep in mind our points above about the themes in the school you select. While all seven of the knowledge areas need to be covered on an accredited degree, different schools will emphasize more or less on specific areas.

In the UK, degrees are modular. That means that you will follow a number of taught modules in which you learn about knowledge areas and other content. You may have the option to select some modules as well as following the core-required modules.

The taught component of a Master's programme typically represents two-thirds of the programme.

The remaining third of the degree consists of a research dissertation. It is a requirement of accredited programmes in Occupational Psychology that students complete a major independent project, in the form of research that involves fieldwork of an applied nature. The dissertation is an extremely valuable opportunity for you to specialize and develop advanced knowledge about an area of the profession that really interests you. Use the opportunity to your advantage. Box 5.2 presents an in-focus guide to completing your Masters dissertation.

Box 5.2 The Masters dissertation

The Masters Dissertation is the area of the Stage 1 training in OP over which you have the most freedom and control. You can research any relevant area of OP, and specialize at quite some depth. You will have the opportunity to work with a supervisor among the academic faculty of your University, and you will develop a close working relationship with them. Completing the research dissertation requires dedication and commitment. There are some things that you can do to help navigate through the process smoothly though.

First, prepare early. Before you arrive at your MSc, look through the backgrounds of all staff in the Department and see if any of their work captures your interest. Start reading in more depth about areas that interest you as soon as you begin your studies, and be proactive in asking staff for recommendations for reading if their area of research is relevant. Select your topic to be relevant to the area you think you may wish to work after your MSc. This will provide good evidence of your skills specialization and give you something relevant to talk about with prospective employers.

A second area of preparation is to think about potential places in which you could conduct your research. You will need to do fieldwork which means collecting data from organizations and employed adults, and not from other students. Your easiest route to finding an organization is to use personal connections, for example family members or friends who work in an organization can help you gain access. If you are undertaking quantitative work, anticipate that you will need at least around 120–150 participants to complete surveys, usually in the region of 10–15 minutes each. For qualitative work, again a typical data collection effort would be 15–20 interviews of around 45–60 minutes. Your contacts need to stretch to permitting this, otherwise you will need to contact other organizations to help.

When you design your project, you should strive to make a research and applied contribution. That is, you will gain better grades if your work addresses a genuine gap in the literature (not a major gap, perhaps you can replicate research in a new setting or culture, for example), whilst also having applied value. Such projects fulfil both academic and practice requirements of your training. You should also think methodologically. Students invariably struggle if they have conceptual ideas that are disconnected from the methods used to study them. In short, if you have ideas, but not understanding about how you could test them, your project is going to be a difficult journey. Think through your ideas logically in terms of the ways in which you can research them practically. Books or Chapters on research methods are a big help (e.g. Woods & West, 2014; Coolican, 2017; Saunders, Lewis, & Thornhill, 2016).

Remember that you cannot collect any of your data before you have been through an ethical review process for your research. Your supervisor will help. When you get to the data collection phase however, expect that it will twice as difficult as you antici-pated. People at work are busy and may not share your enthusiasm for the work you are doing. It is perfectly normal, and not at all personal if they do not fill out your survey. Simply work profession-ally with participating organizations. That means communicating, delivering things when you commit to, being polite with actual participants, and providing the organization with some anony-mized write up of what you found and the implications for them.

Through the course of the year, work steadily on your disserta-tion. You can always be working on a literature review, reading and referencing, and aspects of the methodology section before you collect data. This avoids a later summer dissertation "binge"/panic as the deadline approaches. This will also typically mean better and more valuable interactions with your supervisor, who is not also being contacted by four or five other students in a similar position.

Write you project up as if you were writing for a good academic journal such as the Journal of Occupational and Organizational Psychology. Read similar articles to your research projects and use them as a structural template for your write-up. You could also set this peer-review standard as a benchmark for the quality of the work you produce. Students regularly produce publishable qual-ity dissertations, which can be presented at conferences, or even in journals. It is highly unlikely that the dissertation itself is ready for publication, but if you undertook the research effectively, it is entirely possible that the project can be written up for a jour-nal submission. For two examples of publishable quality student projects, see Woods and Sofat (2013) on work engagement, and Darviri and Woods (2006) on absenteeism. These articles will also give an excellent idea about the scope of the work you will need to do for your dissertation.

Stage 2: supervised practice and the qualification in Occupational Psychology

The Stage 2 of the Qualification in Occupational Psychology (QOcc-Psych) is the part that, once complete, enables you to gain Chartered Membership of the Society, Full Membership of the Division of Occupational Psychology (DOP) and eligibility to apply for registration with the Health and Care Professions Council (HCPC).

There is extensive documentation about the procedures and regulations of completing the QOccPsych, and Stage 2 in particular available at the BPS, and it is not our intention here to simply restate all of it. Rather, we will focus on the key points, the headline requirements of the qualification, and importantly, provide a practical insight from our experience about how to work through the qualification.

A first priority before you commence the qualification is to read all the relevant documentation available to you in detail, so that you are clear about the requirements of the BPS. Take time to clarify anything you are unsure about.

The Stage 2 qualification is unlike most other programmes you may have followed in that you are wholly personally responsible for your own learning and professional development.

The basics of the QOccPsych

Before getting into the detail, here are the headline key points of the Stage 2 of QOccPsych:

- The qualification takes a minimum of 2 years, but you can elect to complete it in three or four years depending on the work you are doing.
- You register and pay programme fees to the BPS directly.
- The format of the programme is supervised practice – that means that you learn through working as a Trainee Occupational Psychologist, supervised by a registered BPS supervisor. Your supervisor does not need to work directly with you, or in the same

organization, but is there to ensure your training progresses effectively. You must meet at least four times per year with your supervisor and have monthly contact.

● Your practice as a psychologist will involve working on a variety of different areas of practice.

● You are assessed regularly through submission of a portfolio of evidence. These detail the work you have undertaken and how you have developed and demonstrated your skills and competencies as a psychologist.

Structure of the programme: content framework

The framework of the content of the Stage 2 is based around two main components:

● Practice of Occupational Psychology leading to competency development

● An applied research project carried out in the course of applied practice

At Stage 2, the BPS define five areas of practice of Occupational Psychology. You must demonstrate that you have practiced in all of them. The five areas are shown in Table 5.1.

In each of the five areas, you must complete substantive pieces of work, and write up a reflective account to submit for assessment. The write-ups must show that you have met certain developmental criteria (more on that shortly).

Table 5.1 The five areas or practice of Occupational Psychology

Psychological assessment at work
Learning, training and development
Leadership, engagement and motivation
Well-being and work
Work design, organizational change and development

You should be able to show a high degree of competence in three specific areas of Occupational Psychology, evidenced by at least three major projects. One of these must be focused on applied research.

It should be clear that there is a higher expectation for the magnitude of the work at the end of Stage 2 as compared to the beginning. However, in all cases, it is important that you are able to show that you have led specific projects or tasks that are meaningful and substantive.

For example, working to deliver a training course is not sufficient on its own as evidence of developing competencies. Rather, you would need to show how the training was identified as a solution to a client need, how it was designed to suit the participants and their needs, and how you evaluated its impact.

Likewise, simply administering psychometric testing for selection would not be substantive enough for your logbook. Instead, you would need to show how you analysed the job criteria to choose the assessment tools, how you communicated results, and evaluated the outcomes of the selection assessment.

In short, the work you submit must show that you are developing your competencies towards being an independent practitioner.

Structure of the programme: competencies and skills

The activities and content requirements of the Stage 2 are the means by which you develop your skills and competencies.

The skills and competencies frameworks also act as assessment criteria for your Stage 2. In the submission write-ups that you produce, you must ensure that you have supplied clear evidence of how you have demonstrated all of the skills and competencies. What are the skills and competencies you need to develop?

There are two main sets of criteria: Occupational Standards and the 'consultancy cycle'. There are four Occupational Standards:

- Standard 1: Ethical, reflective and legal practice
- Standard 2: Competent practice across the five core areas of Occupational Psychology

- Standard 3: Taking an evidence-based approach
- Standard 4: Competency in applying the consultancy cycle

For the purposes of Stage 2, the consultancy cycle is structured around six steps:

1 Contracting
2 Information gathering and analysis of issues
3 Using an evidence-based approach to formulate plans and actions
4 Implementing and reviewing solutions
5 Evaluating outcomes
6 Reporting and reflecting on outcomes

Whatever length of time you elect to take to complete the Stage 2 qualification, your competencies will be assessed based on three submissions of evidence. These become progressively more in-depth and complex as the work you carry out becomes more detailed.

The first submission is formative, which means that it is not assessed, but rather is designed to allow you to receive feedback on the quality of what you have done. This will help you with the subsequent submissions. In this first submission, you will write up one piece of work covering one or two of the core areas of Occupational Psychology. This work must cover mainly Stages 2, 3, 4 and 6 of the consultancy cycle.

The second submission is designed to show that you have covered the full set of five areas of Occupational Psychology. You will submit a portfolio of at least two reports (and most likely more) that covers all of the remaining core areas. Each piece of work that you report should again cover Stages 2, 3, 4, and 6 of the consultancy cycle. You will also include in this submission an outline of the applied research that you plan to carry out.

The third submission is the most detailed and comprises three reports covering three of the core areas of Occupational Psychology. One of the reports must cover Stages 2–6 of the consultancy cycle and the other two reports must cover all six stages. Of these two reports, one is a write-up of the applied research you will have carried out.

Across all of your supervised practice activity, you must demonstrate Occupational Standards 1 and 3. This means that these standards must be evident in the write-ups of your work that you submit for assessment.

Box 5.3 Summary Requirements for the Stage 2 QOccPsych

Submission 1: Formative Assessment

- One report covering up to two core areas of Occupational Psychology (write-up is maximum of 3000 words).

Submission 2: Formative Submission

- At least two reports (maximum 3000 words per report) covering all areas of Occupational Psychology not covered in Submission 1.
- Research outline and ethical review of proposed research.

Submission 3: Final Submission

- Reports of three pieces of applied work.
- Two reports of maximum 4000 words detailing substantial applied practice.
- One report writing up applied research (of around 12000–15000 words).

Viva-voce Assessment

- A viva assessment (essentially a face-to-face interview with an assessor) to review the full set of undertaken work and answer questions about what you done and how you have developed.

The applied research project is the most detailed piece of applied practice work that you submit for assessment at Stage 2. This is not designed to replicate the MSc dissertation and is rather set up to show that you use research skills in the service of consulting practice as a psychologist.

This means that rather than approach the research project from the perspective of academic novelty, you would instead undertake research that provides practical insight and benefit for your consulting work. The research must provide insight that is built into your applied work with clients.

The research might represent a specific step in a client project that involved for example the gathering of primary data to inform solutions. Perhaps data on stress and well-being were collected and analysed to create interventions for a specific organization for example. However, you will need to demonstrate in the submission that you competently carry out and report the research in full.

The full framework of requirements is available from the BPS website (see www.bps.org.uk). Our advice is to use this information carefully to critically review the Stage 2 work you are undertaking. It is a good idea to review each submission to ensure that you have met the relevant criteria and requirements of each, before submitting for assessment.

Before enrolling on the stage 2 programme

Once you attained the Graduate Membership of the BPS (after completing an accredited first degree) and completed an accredited Masters in Occupational Psychology, you are eligible to enrol on the QOcc-Psych Stage 2. But, let's be honest, there is no point being enrolled on the Stage 2 qualification longer than you need to be. Although the programme can be completed in 2 years, most people take 3 years or longer. There are a few activities that you need to work on however, before you enrol. Taking your time to do these thoroughly will make the process smoother and more efficient.

Formulate a Training Plan. When you start the programme, it is best to have a clear idea about how you are going to fulfil all the requirements. Covering the practice areas requires that you are in a job role that will enable you work across all five practice domains. If you cannot cover them all in your job, then you need to have some idea how you can undertake wider work activity to cover them (e.g. external work, voluntary work etc).

You could also have selected which of the areas of practice you will focus on in third submission, and have specific plans for the work that you will undertake. We would recommend that you do not enrol and commence the QOccPsych stage 2 until you are sure that you will be able to undertake substantive work to cover the content of the programme.

Find a Supervisor. The BPS has a register of qualified and approved supervisors. You can search for a supervisor who is local to you. It is a good idea to meet face-to-face with your supervisor to see if you think you'll work well together, and it is also possible to meet potential supervisors at the Annual Division of Occupational Psychology conference. Working effectively with your supervisor will make a big difference to your experience of Stage 2. Remember that at this stage of your training, the responsibility for guiding the process is with you personally. The supervisor is not there to manage or lead you, rather to advise, and facilitate your development. There is more information about how best to work with your supervisor in the box feature.

It is a requirement that you meet your supervisor quarterly to review your training and progress, and have contact monthly. The format of these meetings, and the format and process of recording the meetings should be included in your contract.

Formalise your Plan and Supervision: To enrol on Stage 2, you will need to write a formal plan of development and agree it with your supervisor. You will also need to sign a contract that officially engages your supervisor to oversee your training. If they are external to your employer, the supervisor will also carry out a visit to your place of work to verify that your work and environment and employment are safe, and conducive to completing your training.

Box 5.4 Supervisor site visit, and training plan

Planning your training & work premise risk assessment

The QOccPsych training board at the BPS needs to be confident that you are working in a safe and secure environment. To ensure this the board has set a mandatory requirement that you, your supervisor visit your workplace prior to your enrolment (unless they are internal to your organization). This is to ensure adequate risk assessment is conducted. Your coordinating supervisor is also required to visit your working premises once per year to update the risk assessment as part of the annual progress report.

Producing your plan of training

To produce your plan of training it is critical you work closely with your supervisor to help formulate a well thought out, and structured plan. This plan should show how you are going to apply the knowledge that you previous gained during Stage 1 into a working/ professional environment. Remember the purpose of the plan of training is to demonstrate to the QOccPsych board of assessors how you intend to develop, and demonstrate your ability in the core competencies and skills during your supervised practice. The plan should give the board confidence that you will develop the core competencies and skills of the QOccPsych in reasonable time that you will develop in the way required for independent practice as an Occupational Psychologist.

Your plan should contain adequate detail on how you will use your work role and work opportunities to support your training. To do this, it is critical that you are in a position that makes available to you a sufficient number, duration and range of experiences and opportunities. Your role should complement the supervised practice and provide adequate opportunities to learn and develop, and achieve the learning outcomes.

Box 5.5 Supervisor, coordinating supervisor, designated supervisor?

For simplicity, in this Chapter, we simply refer to a supervisor as a supervisor. However, the Stage 2 process allows that you might have a main "Coordinating Supervisor", who appoints a "Designated Supervisor" (sort of like an assistant supervisor) to help facilitate certain aspects of your training (for example providing workplace support or opportunities to carry out research). It is important to note a Designated Supervisor could be another psychologist or an appropriately qualified HR, coaching or training specialist.

*Make Sure you Complete Logbook Entries for any Relevant Work **Before** you Enrol on the Programme.* This is a really smart move to make. In the search for the perfect job that enables you to do fulfil requirements of covering all of the practice areas, it is possible that you will have undertaken some relevant work along the way.

Upon enrolment for the Stage 2, you will have the opportunity to submit evidence of existing skills and competencies developed through work already undertaken. This means that you can use this experience to form the first submission for the programme (Submission 1).

To be eligible for inclusion in the portfolio though, the work must be post-Stage 1 (i.e. after the Master's degree) and supervised by a qualified and registered Occupational Psychologist.

In short, you need to be proactive to make this happen. Before you enrol on the Stage 2, if you perceive that a work assignment might be eligible to include in your portfolio of competence, you should ensure that you identify a registered Occupational Psychologist who can supervise your work on the activity. They do not need to continue to supervise you formally beyond the specific piece of work, but it is essential that you have supervision while you are working on it.

Programme enrolment

Once you have all of the pre-enrolment tasks completed and in order, you are ready to enrol formally on the programme.

Some final things that you will need to make your application:

- An enhanced CRB (criminal record background) check
- Names of two references, one of whom must be a registered Occupational Psychologist
- A health reference (this is a Health and Care Professions Council requirement; see the BPS website).

The assessment process: annual review

Once on the programme, in addition to your formal submissions your progress is assessed annually. At the end of each year of your registration on the programme, you will submit an annual report for BPS-accredited assessors to review.

The annual report may comprise for examples:

- Annual workplace review (included updated risk assessment)
- Supervisor's evaluation of the trainee's competence and development
- Supervisory meeting records
- Updated plan of training, indicating completed work and any amendments

Assessment of competence

Your skills and competencies are assessed through review of your portfolio: three submissions plus the viva assessment at the end.

Assessors will review each of your written submissions, and will decide if the evidence you have supplied demonstrates the skills and competencies satisfactorily. They may provide feedback asking you to clarify or provide more detail on some elements, for which you will be able to respond, or incorporate into future submissions. The final submission is especially important and depending upon the outcome, you may need to undertake further work, or proceed to the viva.

The viva is a face-to-face interview designed to explore the final submission in more depth. The purpose is to allow discussion and clarification of any aspects the assessors would like more detail about, and to assure them that you have developed as indicated by the written submission, and that you have carried out the work that you report. It is the final means by which your competence as a psychologist is assessed.

The task of the assessor is ultimately to establish if you have demonstrated competence, and that you are fit to practice as an independent Occupational Psychologist. At that time, they will recommend to the QOccPsych board that you be awarded the qualification, and it is time for you to celebrate!

Registering with the HCPC as an Occupational Psychologist

Having worked long and hard to attain the QOccPsych, you will want to use your new professional title of Occupational Psychologist. To do so, your final step is to register with Health and Care Professions Council (HCPC).

Once qualified, the registration process is straightforward. You will have already demonstrated your fitness to practice, so this stage is rather a formality. Nevertheless, registration is a significant transition, from trainee, to full practitioner psychologist. With the registration comes new accountability. Your clients will be reassured that you are professionally regulated, and that there is a professional body to whom you are accountable and answerable.

Another responsibility that you will have is for your own professional development. As an OP, you will always be learning, and the programme of training that you follow will help you develop a natural inclination towards continuing your professional development. As a scientific discipline, OP is always advancing and the intersection of our techniques with technology and societal change makes the profession dynamic. As part of your ongoing and long-term registration with as a practitioner psychologist, there is a requirement to undertake *continuing professional development* (CPD), and to keep a record of it. However for a competent OP, the requirement should really only recognize the continuous learning that they are already doing. It is a professional responsibility as well as a regulatory obligation.

Starting-out and managing your trajectory

Graduates of MSc OP programmes enter a competitive market for jobs. In this Chapter, we will cover some general advice on starting successfully in OP as a career, and look at how to craft your experience for two different kinds of employer: consultancies and larger corporates or public organizations. We will also reflect on how to make your career in OP a rewarding one, by creating personal value in the way you develop and apply your skills as a psychologist.

At the outset, we first want to dispel a myth; that experience is essential to get a job in OP. It isn't. The caveat though is that you need to be an exceptional individual in order to get a job without experience. If your academic achievements and ability are exceptional, and your communication and interpersonal skills are also excellent, then it is perfectly possible that you would be hired into a trainee OP or junior consultant role.

At the same time, we want to manage your expectations appropriately. Exceptional is exactly what it means: an exception to the norm. Such individuals are quite rare, from our experience of education, perhaps 1 or 2 in every 50 graduates fall into this category. So, in all likelihood, you will need experience in order to start out as an OP.

Getting experience is a challenge for everybody. OPs are particularly likely to fall into the common catch 22 situation of entering the working world – employers want work experience, but students cannot therefore get experience without experience. The highly academic route to the MSc means that the situation is especially acute for OPs. The length of time for which trainees find themselves in this situation is however, within their control to some degree, and a positive proactive approach, starting as early as possible, will give an advantage. The next section considers the kind of positive work experience that you might acquire.

Work experience pre-masters

By the time you reach the halfway point on an MSc in OP, you will be in the process of applying for your first job. MSc programmes are exceptionally demanding, especially when compared to Bachelors programmes, and so with the tasks of job searching and applications, working on assignments and dissertations, and having a social life, the opportunity to build up great work experience is limited. This is why we focus here on work experience pre-MSc.

There is an old adage that all work experience is good, whether you work in a shop, a restaurant, at a leisure centre and so on. It is true to some extent that having a job shows that you can be self-disciplined enough to be employed. However, that is as far as this really stretches in the context of a career in OP. Work experience in OP needs to provide prospective employers with confidence of your professional credibility and effectiveness.

OP is a professional discipline. Most OPs work in professional settings therefore, working from an office environment base, and interacting with clients who, for the most part, are from similarly professional backgrounds. Clients are also working *adults*. Your work experience needs to reflect this. Furthermore, there are some things to keep in mind about how to turn adequate work experience into excellent.

Adequate work experience would show that you have made an effective contribution in a professional office environment. For example, experience as an office temp or administrator would show that you are organized, that you can support more senior colleagues, use IT and email, and maintain a professional approach in a relevant work environment. Medium or larger companies tend to offer better experience, as you will work with a wider variety of other people, developing your communication skills.

Good work experience is more immediately relevant to the work on OPs. An example would be work in a human resource department.

Human resource (HR) professionals are key clients of OPs, they study similar areas of practice and are concerned with the kind of people management questions that concern us. The degree of co-working is such that OPs and HR practitioners might be considered professional partners in some respects.

Experience in a HR department would be good experience because you would encounter some of the key personnel activities that OPs get involved in. For example, recruitment and selection, training and development, performance appraisal and management, well-being and stress management and so on. The work could involve making preparations for these kinds of activities, associated administration and keeping records. However, there would also likely be some interactions with the management or departments that use the HR services. This interaction is effective preparation for working with client in the future, as you will get a sense of their needs and requirements.

Another type of "good" work experience is research work in an academic setting. These opportunities typically come in the second or final years of your bachelors education, although you could possibly get some experience even before University. Work of this kind is data-focused, but that does not necessarily mean computer working exclusively. It is likely that you would be asked to work on data input, but also you could be asked to collect data, by collecting surveys, interviewing participants, or carrying out procedures or experiments.

In academic research, these activities come under the title of research assistance. So, don't expect that you would be leading on a research project or academic journal paper. Rather, you are supporting an academic in the pursuit of their own research. You can still however gain a lot of benefit, if you try to ensure that you keep regular communication with the academic, be open for calls or meetings to learn from them, and try to understand the research that you are doing, as well as following the protocols you are given.

Academic research experience is valuable in OP, because you can apply what you learn in your MSc research project or dissertation, and take the skills beyond your education and into your work as an OP. Research assistant experience is also especially valuable if you think you may want to undertake further study such as a PhD, and ultimately be an academic working in a University in the future.

Excellent work experience

Great or excellent work experience should enable you to develop background skills and competencies that enhance your profile beyond your education. There are two specific kinds of experience that we would classify as "excellent". The first is sales in the context of business consulting. Recruitment consultancies or agencies are highly performance oriented cultures generally. Internships or junior roles typically involve resourcing (seeking out and qualifying potential clients), and dealing with prospective candidates (administrative support). If you are able to take a role as an actual consultant, all the better, as you will be held to more stretching sales objectives. The key is that you are held responsible for delivering a volume of business.

Why is this "excellent" experience? It is not necessarily that you are learning best practice in recruitment. Rather, you are learning how to independently develop consultancy income to contribute to a business. Occupational Psychology consultancy requires selling and business development skills as well as technical skills for project delivery. Your education is arguably much better at preparing you for the latter and is rather weaker at preparing you for sales type work. It is always encouraging to see a good record of performance and employment in a target-oriented environment, as it shows that you can independently contribute to an OP consultancy business.

The second type of "excellent experience", is experience specifically in an OP consultancy or with a group of OPs in a company. This experience will enable you to see first-hand the work the OPs get involved in. Internship work may again be administrative, resourcing, or research work, and are valuable because you will have an understanding of how OP teams operate, and you may even pick up technical and delivery skills through project work or contact with clients. It is a good idea to check what you would be doing during an internship with an OP firm before applying, and particularly whether you would be able to learn from more experienced practitioners. Because OP consultancies are small typically, accessibility of key people in the company could be limited, and you may be working remotely for a portion of your time.

Whatever your experience, it is a good idea to proactively manage your own development. Some tips for this are shown in Box 6.1.

Box 6.1 Managing your internship manager

The quality of your experience on an internship depends greatly on your initiative, and how you manage your manager and your own learning. HR experience is a good illustrative example because it has the potential to offer more due to the capacity to craft roles within most HR departments. The idea of job crafting is, interestingly, a current area of research in work and organizational psychology. The notion is that some people, given the right job environment, and autonomy within it, have the opportunity to mould or *craft* their job description to fit their strengths and the things that they enjoy or want to do to help their career. The HR function in an organization is often wide-ranging and the kinds of activities undertaken are such that it is possible to experience a varied portfolio of tasks and assignments. This is all positive for developing your CV, knowledge and basic skills relevant to OP.

However, crafting is not a right, it must be earned. Students would be advised to know when and how to engage in crafting to improve the quality of the work experience. A good strategy is to treat job experience in a way that enables you to understand *the lay of the land* before taking steps to change it.

For example, do what you are asked to do firstly and foremostly, and do it solidly and effectively. While you are building dependability into your record, observe. Look around and understand who does what, who knows who, who are the key people who could help with your experience (i.e. people you may like to work with). Get a feel for how decisions are made, what scope there is for people to try new things, take on developmental tasks and innovate. Once you are *settled*, that is once you have proven yourself capable of delivering what has been asked (probably after around 10–12 weeks), then is the right time to begin crafting.

Approach your line manager and ask for a review meeting to get some feedback on your performance, and talk about your development. Be prepared to listen to the feedback and respond with ideas about how you could improve further. Have in your mind some potential activities that you feel would be developmental. For example, have you seen colleagues working on a relevant or interesting project? Are there regular interesting days or events that you would like to support? Ask if there could be an opportunity to work on some of those activities. Importantly, reassure your line manager that you will take care to manage your time so that your core responsibilities are not affected. If you have chance to work on some of the things you would like, treat them as opportunities to learn: listen, observe and again, get a feel for the new demands.

From one perspective, you might think this strategy sounds like taking on extra work for no reward. If so, your perception is wrong. This is because the experience you get as a result will be much more valuable, and so you are increasing the intangible rewards of the work significantly. Moreover, if you do these interesting things well you will quickly be assigned to more complex roles, not for just your own benefit, but for your employer's too.

The final point on managing your manager and your own learning is knowing when to move on. At some stage you may find that the returns you are getting for your effort in an internship are becoming marginal. You may not be getting the learning opportunities you want, and you may not be earning enough money to compensate. So, know when is the right time to move on. If your manager is not open to enriching your experience, and you feel that you have earned some additional capacity and responsibility by showing effectiveness in your work, then it may be the right time. If you think that you have all the experience and skills development you can get from a role, then you may wish to try something else. The only caveat is that in our view, you are probably still learning after a year or more, even if you may not immediately perceive it. Also, the context of your overall work profile makes a difference, because having many short-term roles, especially if they are not fixed-term internships, creates a poor impression on your CV concerning commitment and application.

What are employers looking for?

What should be implicit in this Chapter so far is that employers in OP are looking for a combination of different skills and competencies. Earlier Chapters should enable you to see that being an OP requires extensive preparation and training, and so we would consider the career and profession to be complex compared to many other career options. We know from our work as OPs that complex jobs necessarily require multiple skills and competencies in order to fulfil those requirements. We are also at an advantage though in terms of understanding how to make sense of the competencies of OP, enabling you to understand where you have strengths and development needs.

The most straightforward way to divide the competencies is to think about the differences between core and technical sides. Starting with the technical side, which cuts across all specialisms of OP, employers are looking for a distinctive and extensive capability from your MSc OP degree. This means that they are interested by how you have ensured depth of learning and understanding, how your degree has been specialized by your University, and the ways in which you have differentiated yourself from every other OP graduate. You must not only cover the skills and knowledge of OP as reviewed in Chapter 2, but also develop some depth of knowledge in specific areas.

Specialization is key to developing distinctive technical competencies. As you proceed through your MSc, you should consider what kind of job you would like post-completion and develop your technical understanding and competencies accordingly. So, if you would like to work in psychometrics, it would be a good idea to focus on understanding methods programmes. You could seek out extra support from you lecturers and tutors to develop skills in reliability testing, factor analysis and structural equation modelling. Next, you could undertake your dissertation in the same area, and strive for a publishable-quality scientific study. Showing you can design research in a way that could stand up to peer-review gives a vote of confidence to your technical competencies.

Alongside the technical competencies are core competencies. These are general competencies that are relevant not just to OP, but to the working world more widely. Their relevance to a given career path in OP will vary, but there are key commonalities nevertheless. For example, planning and organization is critical in all situations, especially because OPs tend to work on project-type work, and often work on different things at the same time. Problem solving and analysis also feature heavily in the approach that OPs take to consultancy. Resilience and communication skills represent two general areas of personal effectiveness that you can assume are essential for finding employment.

Then there are the kinds of competencies that were highlighted in the potential work experience areas that we reviewed. These include business acumen, and sales and marketing skills. There will be some variation in the extent to which these are needed by employers. However, it is a safe assumption that if you are going into practice as a consultant, understanding of critical business issues will be relevant and desirable in the eyes of employers.

Speaking from a personal perspective, and returning to our discussion of OP values earlier in the book, a key personal value that essential to employers, especially those that represent the best of OP in practice, is integrity, both ethical and professional.

Ethical integrity is about doing things in ways that meet the expected standards of conduct for psychologists. But, it is also more than this; it is acting in ways that show a commitment and belief in those standards. In ways that indicate that ethics is seen as quality enhancing in our profession, and as making us different from other comparable practitioner professions.

Professional integrity on the other hand is much more about ones identity as a psychologist. It may seem obvious, but if an employer wants to hire a psychologist, then they want that person to have a professional identity as a psychologist, not a generalist consultant. Professional integrity involves working in ways that *apply psychology*. Thinking about applied problems in terms of the psychological implications and factors that need to be considered, how the role of science and evidence need to factor into problem solutions.

Having professional integrity also sometimes involves telling clients, and other people we work with, things that they may not want to hear. A personal reflection serves to highlight this. As a leader in an organization, there is often need to work on personnel activities, not in a consultative sense, but rather as a line manager. One notable experience was a situation of downsizing, where many people's jobs in the organization were at risk. There was a heated meeting in which these issues were discussed by a group of senior management. One group head objected to the necessary process of requiring people in the organization to apply for their jobs, an established fair and transparent process for managing redundancy. He rather wanted to select those people that he thought were the better performers based on his own perceptions. In this situation, I (i.e. one of the authors) spoke up, and explained why fair and systematic selection was needed in order to provide each person with an opportunity to have their capability effectively assessed. The case made was based on best practice in selection from a psychological point of view. The lesson is that being a manager, does not stop one being a psychologist, and specifically a professional OP.

A second example concerned student recruitment. It was proposed that one business programme introduced interviewing as part of the ways in which students would be offered places on the programme. However, it was not clear how students would be assessed, what capabilities would be measured and why. It also seemed that the ways that students presented themselves could potentially play a big part in the decision. Again, in this situation, it was important to be a psychologist, and share concerns about bias, stereotyping, and possible impact on the opportunity of students from diverse backgrounds joining the programme. It was difficult to give this message, although once the concerns were communicated, several others in the group were given confidence to also voice similar opinions. It was proposed that a structured assessment via interview would be needed to ensure fairness if implemented.

Professional integrity as an OP is a highly desirable characteristic to employers. Our professional values need to be enabling in the sense that they focus on showing clients and other stakeholders how psychology can be used to help then do things in better ways than they might otherwise do, even if the message is difficult.

In short, employers are looking for technically competent, credible and personally effective, professional trainee OPs. You do not need to be the "finished article" when you leave University, but you must show in words, actions and interactions, that you fit with this level of expectation.

Getting hired

Once you have acquired the kind of profile that we have described in terms of experience, skills and competencies, the next challenge is to get your first job as an OP. Having the competencies and skills is, like in any other competitive industry, not the whole story in terms of getting a job.

OPs are selection experts. That means that in order to get hired into an OP consultancy or group, you can expect a stretching and rigorous assessment process. The context of assessment and selection is also arguably more conventionally like a business or corporate process than other psychology specialisms. Our advice in this section reflects this. Typically, selection into trainee roles comprise a number of selection activities and stages:

1   Application Form: The application form is likely to go beyond simple reporting of education and employment background. Rather you can expect that you will be requested to provide information about key experiences from you education or work experience that illustrate your competencies. There are ways to present this information that will give you the best opportunity of being shortlisted (see section below). The application form is also important in terms of ensuring that you give the right account of the work experience you have acquired. Be sure to include information about key projects and contributions, and any training that you undertook.

2   Psychometric Testing: Absolutely to be expected, given that designing them is core business for OPs, psychometric tests will factor strongly in decisions to move applicants through to the later selection stages. You will likely be asked to complete two forms of psychometric, personality and reasoning ability tests. If you have not had experience of completing tests before, it is a good idea to try to get some experience through your University careers service, or you can visit the British Psychological Society's Psychological Testing Centre online to find some resources about tests and how they work.

For the personality testing side, it is simply important that you complete the assessment honestly and accurately. There is nothing to be gained in trying to "game" the assessment in any way. Most profiles allow for faking to be identified and checked, and hiring firms will quickly see through any impression management at later stages of the assessment. Take care though to think about how you have developed through your education and training, focusing on what you typically do in your work and professional life. This will ensure the most accurate picture is presented of your potential.

For the ability testing, practice is advised. This is not because it gives you an advantage. Rather, being unfamiliar with testing puts you at a disadvantage. That is, you are unlikely to be able to show your full potential if part of your cognitive ability is spent figuring out how the test items are set out. The best strategy with most psychometric tests of ability is to work quickly and accurately. You will not do well by guessing answers, even if they are multiple choice. An index of accuracy may be computed for example. However, if you agonise over your responses to individual questions, it is highly likely that you will score lower on the tests because your progress through the items is slow. Give yourself the best chance by answering quickly and accurately.

3   The Assessment Centre: Assessment centres (ACs) for OPs will usually be a whole day process. The day will comprise you working on a variety of activities. By the time you reach the AC, you will already be an expert in their design and validity, having covered them on your Masters programme. The technical part, we will therefore spare you.

The AC exercises could include a group exercise in which your interpersonal competencies are assessed, and a role play activity in which you are asked to conduct a one-to-one discussion. A standard activity for prospective OPs however will be a presentation of some form, likely set in the context of presenting to a client. This is where your credibility and communication with clients will be determined. If you are not a competent presenter (be self-critical, it is not everybody's strength), then it is a good idea to practice with some peers or attend a presentation skills course. This is because your presentation performance will make or break your prospects of being hired to a significant degree.

During the AC, be professional and pleasant with assessors and other candidates. Remember that OP is a relatively small industry, and even if you are not hired, you will likely meet people who may be future colleagues, clients, or employers. Be yourself, but your professional self, again keeping your training in mind, and your values as a psychologist centre of your approach.

4   Interviews: Interviews will be structured, meaning that you will be asked standardized questions, possibly competency-type questions. There could be space for some more general questions about your past experience, aspirations or motivation, but one would expect that if you are being hired by an OP, they would adopt a structured approach to their interviewing. Forget what you have seen in popular culture (e.g. *the Apprentice*) about how interviews proceed. It is not an adversarial experience, if it is, think twice about joining the organization. Instead, you should communicate clearly and concisely about your experiences to demonstrate how your competencies have enabled you to perform. Concrete examples of experience are almost always more compelling evidence than general assertions about your views or preferred approaches. Within the answers you give to questions, there is an effective format to use to frame your competencies (see below).

A further tip with interviews, which is often proposed, but not often followed: know the organization or company to which you are applying. Learn as much about them as possible from the internet, social media, and other research. Try to know already about their priorities and services, and get a sense of their values from the way in which communication and media are presented. Work out for yourself how you can contribute, and ensure this comes through in your answers to interview questions.

Finally, some of the most impressive candidates for interview are those that follow up post interview to thank assessors for the experience. As a hiring manager, the level of work and preparation from the employer side to organize an AC and selection process can be underestimated. It creates an excellent impression to receive a personal email thanking the team if the experience you had as a candidate was a good one. If you meet specific people, remember who they were, make a note of what you talked about, and send them a personal email to thank them for their time and the discussion you had with them. Do not try in any way to influence their decision-making, instead simply thank them and say that you look forward to receiving their feedback.

The advice we provide here is a reflection on our experience as recruiters and assessors of OPs, and based on how we see students enter the jobs market post-MSc. If you have well-developed competencies, and navigate the assessments taking some of our advice, you will be in a good position to start out in OP.

However, we also want your expectations to be realistic; getting hired can be hard work, especially if your experiences are unsuccessful in the early stages post-MSc. Rejection is draining for everybody, despite the positive spin that one may put on it. Here is a professional truth though that has played out over multiple years of experience of training and working with OPs. Everyone finds a job. The search may be longer for some people compared to others, but all OP graduates do end up working in some role that enables them to apply their skills in some form.

How to present evidence of your competencies

Whether in writing or in face-to-face communication, you will give yourself an advantage in getting into an OP career by knowing how to present your competencies in the right way. Assessors will expect a particular format of the answers to help them understand your potential, so it is a good recommendation to make their job as straightforward as possible by giving them the information they need. As mentioned earlier, prioritize evidence of what you have actually done in your experience. Examples of specific projects or activities are valued most highly by recruiters. Then, in presenting the evidence of your experience, follow a format that enables the maximum detail to be presented. The STAR model is an effective way to do this:

Situation: Provide a brief account of the background to the situation and the aspects that factored in your experience. This will help the interviewer to understand the relevance of your experience.

Task: Here, describe the specific task that you worked on in the focal situation. What were you required to do? What were the objectives? What was the purpose of the task that you worked on?

Action: This is a critical section and should comprise at least half of your answer to an interview question. Specifically, here you would describe what you *did* in the situation in response to the task demands. Competency assessment is behavioural and assessors will look for evidence of the behaviours that you demonstrated in your experience. The assessment methodology involves cross-referencing the evidence you provide against the competencies for the role. We gave indication earlier of the kinds of competencies that are valuable in OP, so keep in mind how your experience can demonstrate them.

Result: At the end of the example you are describing, you should provide some information about the outcome and result. What did you and your team achieve as a consequence of the actions you took? Be clear about where outcomes were positive, and any further actions that you took if they were not.

This same format works well in interviews, or application forms where you need to present evidence of your experience. You can improve your approach still further if you plan a set of key experiences that you can present as examples.

Your personal professional value: the career enabler

OP is a career in which you have substantial control over your career trajectory. You can influence the ways in which your career success plays out, and the rate at which you attain the things that are important to you as an OP. Central to the idea of controlling your career trajectory is the concept of *value*. Your impact and attainment as an OP will be a direct function of your personal value, so what is it? We propose an equation to define it:

Personal Professional Value as an OP = Training as an OP + [(Uniqueness of Skills) × (Applied Need for Skills) × (Social Capital)]

The equation components reflect of course, only a personal professional view about how value is created in the profile of OP.

Training as an OP. This is a constant in the equation, meaning that it is a given that you would have undertaken a programme that covers all of the main areas of OP. The exact value of the training would be different from student to student based on what they studied, where they studied etc. However this is not where the individual value of an OP is created necessarily, rather it comes from the other factors in the equation.

Uniqueness of Skills. Specialization is the key to creating value in your skills as an OP. There are many different applications of the discipline in practice, as you will have learned from this book. No OP can be a true expert in all of them. This is recognized in the training of OPs, which in the BPS Stage 2, progresses towards more in depth practice.

As a practitioner, you are likely to earn income based on your time, which is a finite resource, so really it is important to strive to extract the maximum value out of one hour or unit of your time. The way you can do that is by making your contribution unique. Where you simply offer the same as any other OP or consultant, you compete with them, and market competition tends to push costs and opportunities down. If you have unique knowledge and skills, then by definition, you can offer something that nobody else can. As a consequence your time is more valuable. Decide on what you want to specialize in, and master it.

Applied Need for Skills. Of course, simply knowing how to do something unique is not sufficient to create value. That something unique needs to be valuable to clients. The applied need for the work that you can offer determines if your skills are sought after by clients and keeps you in demand as a practitioner. If you are struggling to convince clients about the need for the services that you can provide, then it is an indicator that the applied need is low. It will suppress your personal value ultimately.

Be aware also that the applied need for your skills is not a constant. For example, skills in designing paper-based psychometrics have been completely devalued in the digital economy, as almost all testing is now online. Tracking and anticipating changes in the value of your unique skills will help to maintain your personal value.

Social Capital. Your unique skills and their applied need are essentially a representation of your *intellectual capital.* However, having high intellectual capital only means that you have potential personal value. That potential will only be realized as a function of your social capital. Social capital is the extent of your interpersonal network, and how much they know about you and your skills as an OP. Much of your work and impact as an OP will come through personal connections, recommendations and relationships with both clients and other practitioners. Allocating time and effort to developing and maintaining your social capital is essential to building your personal professional value.

Social media of course makes this much easier because you are able to stay connected virtually to a broad range of contacts. Although the number of followers in a list is not on its own social capital. Online networking is no substitute for face-to-face networking at conferences, workshops and professional practice events. Participating in these kinds of events is part and parcel of being a member of the OP community, and if you are an active member, the connections you will make will help you move through your career effectively. So, contribute; present your work, tell people about your skills and experiences, help other OPs starting-out to learn.

Personal Professional Value as an OP. As a function of these factors, we propose that you can build and maintain personal professional value as an OP. It is an equation, so that means that value in one area can compensate for another. For example, if your skills are not so specialized, but there is a high applied need, then your value is maintained. If you have high social capital, this can also compensate for lower applied need, or less specialized contributions. The highest professional value is nevertheless achieved when people have an effective combination of all three, and in such cases career trajectories and progression is faster and easier to manage.

What if you do not want to *become an Occupational Psychologist?*

Well, to start with, we will feel a sense of personal responsibility, and a twinge of failure, having possibly put you off the career. But there again, it is probably the case that you knowing this now is a benefit. In this book, we have tried to write with professional integrity in providing a realistic picture of how to become a successful OP in practice. If on reading this, the profession does not seem attractive, then choosing not to be an OP is at least a decision that you take based on sound information.

We would however, not discourage you from studying work and organizational psychology at Bachelors or Masters level. This is because we believe that there is a huge potential for contribution to organizations and management for people who have studied work and organizational psychology. The things you learn about, and the skills you acquire provide important insights and methods of working that are beneficial whether you are working as a psychologist, or simply working in management or in any other role in an organization. The perspective you get from training in psychology will mean you approach your work in a particular way, and you will be able to add something unique as a consequence. In short, you can still use your learning in Occupational Psychology to inform what you do, even if you do not go down the route of training and registering as a practitioner Occupational Psychologist.

Final reflections

Work *matters*. Perhaps more than we fully grasp sometimes. Peter Warr, eminent work psychologist argues that work provides critical benefits to our psychological well-being; what he refers to as "vitamins" for our happiness. They include for example the opportunity for using our skills, for experiencing interpersonal contact, and for attaining a valued social position. Work is singular in providing such a wide array of well-being benefits. Despite the ways in which we sometimes look at our work, it really does make a positive difference to our lives, not just through material benefits, but by fulfilling complex psychological needs to attain competence, social worth, meaningfulness in one's time and activity, and to develop social relationships built around collaboration and cooperation. By becoming an Occupational Psychologist, you will find the opportunity to have all of these benefits yourself of course, but more than this, you will have the chance to make a positive difference to the *work*, and therefore, the *lives* of others. A career in which you can positively influence a feature of everybody's lives that in turn underpins so much of what we do in our societies, cultures and families.

References

Coolican, H. (2017). *Research methods and statistics in psychology*. London: Psychology Press.

Cox, T. (1993). *Stress research and stress management: Putting theory to work* (Vol. 61). Sudbury: HSE Books.

Darviri, S. V., & Woods, S. A. (2006). Uncertified absence from work and the Big Five: An examination of absence records and future absence intentions. *Personality and Individual Differences, 41*(2), 359–369.

Gonzalez, J. A., & Denisi, A. S. (2009). Cross level effects of demography and diversity climate on organizational attachment and firm effectiveness. *Journal of Organizational Behavior, 30*(1), 21–40.

Gottfredson, L. S. (1997). Mainstream science on intelligence: An editorial with 52 signatories, history, and bibliography. *Intelligence, 24*(1), 13–23.

Griffith, R. L., & Wang, M. (2010). The internationalization of IO psychology: We're not in Kansas anymore. *The Industrial-Organizational Psychologist, 48*(1), 41–46.

Humphrey, S. E., Nahrgang, J. D., & Morgeson, F. P. (2007). Integrating motivational, social, and contextual work design features: A meta-analytic summary and theoretical extension of the work design literature. *Journal of Applied Psychology, 92*(5), 1332–1356.

Judge, T. A., Bono, J. E., Ilies, R., & Gerhardt, M. W. (2002). Personality and leadership: A qualitative and quantitative review. *Journal of Applied Psychology, 87*(4), 765–780.

Judge, T. A., Thoresen, C. J., Bono, J. E., & Patton, G. K. (2001). The job satisfaction-job performance relationship: A qualitative and quantitative review. *Psychological Bulletin, 127*(3), 376–407.

Kirkpatrick, D. L. (1976). Evaluation of training. In R. L. Craig (Ed.) *Training and development handbook*. New York: McGraw-Hill.

Kluger, A. N., & DeNisi, A. (1996). The effects of feedback interventions on performance: A historical review, a meta-analysis and a preliminary feedback intervention theory. *Psychological Bulletin, 119*, 254–284.

McKenna, E. F. (2012). *Business psychology and organisational behaviour: A student's handbook*. London: Psychology Press.

Pearn Kandola (2015). *The iLead Model and tools for leadership*. Oxford, UK: Pearn Kandola Publishing.

Robbins, S. P., Judge, T., & Campbell, T. T. (2012). *Organizational behaviour*. Upper Saddle River, NJ: Financial Times/Prentice Hall.

Rousseau, D. M. (2006). Is there such a thing as "evidence-based management"?. *Academy of Management Review*, 31(2), 256–269.

Ryan, M. K., & Haslam, S. A. (2007). The glass cliff: Exploring the dynamics surrounding the appointment of women to precarious leadership positions. *Academy of Management Review*, 32(2), 549–572.

Salas, E., & Cannon-Bowers, J. A. (2001). The science of training: A decade of progress. *Annual Review of Psychology*, 52(1), 471–499.

Saunders, M., Lewis, P., & Thornhill, A. (2016). *Research methods for business students*. London: Pearson Education.

Schaufeli, W. B., Bakker, A. B., & Salanova, M. (2006). The measurement of work engagement with a short questionnaire: A cross-national study. *Educational and Psychological Measurement*, 66(4), 701–716.

West, M. A. (2012). *Effective teamwork: Practical lessons from organizational research*. West Sussex, UK: John Wiley & Sons.

West, M. A., Guthrie, J. P., Dawson, J. F., Borrill, C. S., & Carter, M. (2006). Reducing patient mortality in hospitals: The role of human resource management. *Journal of Organizational Behavior*, 27(7), 983–1002.

Woods, S. A., & Sofat, J. A. (2013). Personality and engagement at work: The mediating role of psychological meaningfulness. *Journal of Applied Social Psychology*, 43(11), 2203–2210.

Woods, S. A., & West, M. A. (2014). *The psychology of work and organizations*. Hampshire, UK: Cengage Learning EMEA.

Woods, S. A., Lievens, F., De Fruyt, F., & Wille, B. (2013). Personality across working life: The longitudinal and reciprocal influences of personality on work. *Journal of Organizational Behavior*, 34(S1), S7–S25.

Index

Note: Page numbers in italic indicate a figure and page numbers in bold indicate a table on the corresponding page